Whiplash and Hidden Soft Tissue Injuries

When, Where and Why to Refer Auto Accident Patients

Second Edition

Dr. R. Jay Shetlin

with Bryan Larson, Esq.

and Dr. Jeffrey A. States

Introduction by Rachot Vacharothone, MD

South Jordan, UT

www.drjayshetlin.com

Copyright ©2013 Dr. R. Jay Shetlin

Conundrum Publishing
10456 S. Redwood Rd.
South Jordan, UT 84095

All rights reserved. No part of this book may be reproduced or transmitted in any form or by any means, electronic or mechanical, including photocopying, recording, or by any information storage and retrieval system without written permission of the publisher, except for the inclusion of brief quotations in a review.

Although the author and publisher have made every effort to ensure the accuracy and completeness of information contained in this book, we assume no responsibility for errors, inaccuracies, omissions, or any inconsistency herein.

Disclaimer

Second Edition

The purpose of the book is to educate. The authors or publisher do not guarantee that anyone following the techniques, suggestions, tips, ideas, or strategies will become successful. The authors and publisher shall have neither liability or responsibility to anyone with respect to any loss or damage caused, or alleged to be caused, directly or indirectly by the information contained in this book.

Printed in the United States of America

Library of Congress Control Number: 2013908565

Book cover and interior design: PairOfAcesDesigns.com

Shetlin, R. Jay.

Whiplash and hidden soft tissue injuries : when, where and why to refer auto accident patients / Dr. R. Jay Shetlin ; with Bryan Larson and Dr. Jeffrey A. States ; introduction by Rachot Vacharothone. -- 2nd ed. -- South Jordan, UT : Conundrum Pub., c2013.

p. ; cm.

ISBN: 978-0-9843900-3-8 (pbk.) ; 978-0-9843900-4-5 (ebook)
Previous edition: 2011.
Summary: With over 3 million whiplash injuries in the US each year, countless individuals suffer from long term/chronic pain and health problems due to improper diagnosis and treatment. Whiplash and hidden soft tissue injuries often require an interdisciplinary health care team approach. Knowing when, where and why to refer auto accident patients is a vital part in helping them receive the best care possible.--Publisher.

1. Whiplash injuries--Treatment. 2. Soft tissue injuries--Treatment. 3. Crash injuries--Treatment. 4. Traffic accident victims--Medical care. 5. Cervical vertebrae--Wounds and injuries--Treatment. 6. Neck--Wounds and injuries--Treatment. I. Larson, Bryan A. II. States, Jeffrey A. III. Title.

RD533.5 .S54 2013
2013908565

617.5/3044--dc23
1308

Dedication

For all those who have lived, loved and lost due to human error or the negligence of others.

Special thanks to – Drs. Arthur Croft, Daniel Murphy and Jeffrey States, for inspiring a profession to transform a specialty to an elevated level of expertise.

Table of Contents

Introduction i
The Modern Hippocratic Oath iii
Glossary of Terms,
Abbreviations, and Symbols iv
**Brief History of Automobile
Development and Injuries** 1
   Evolution Toward Seatbelts and Airbags 2
      Seatbelts 2
      Three-Point Lap and Shoulder Seatbelts 3
      Safety Testing and Airbags 3
   Airbags 4
   Airbag Safety 5
   Brief History of Treatment Guidelines 6
Motor Vehicle Collision Physics 101 9
   Inertia 9
   Change of Velocity 10
   Acceleration 10
   Force 10
   Energy 11
   Momentum 11
   Impulse 11
   G-force or g's 12
   The Laws of Motion and Motor Vehicle Collisions 13
   Mass in Motion 14
      Vehicle Mass and Acceleration force 15
   Low Speed vs. High Speed Collisions 16
   Crumple Zones 17
      Wet or Icy Roads vs. Dry Roads 20
      Vehicle Damage vs. Passenger Injury 22
   Impact Vectors 23
Motor Vehicle Collision Occupant Injuries Anatomy and Physiology 27
   Infant Anatomy 27
   Adult Anatomy 28
   Diagnostic Tools 30
      Static X-ray Film 30
      Digital Motion X-ray 30
      MRI 31
      Physical Examination 32
   Important Factors in Treatment 32
      Blood Vasculature 32
      Inflammation and Scar Tissue 32
      Time Frame of Healing 34
      Ligaments 35
   Anatomy and Physiology in Summary 37
Motor Vehicle Collision Occupant Injuries 38
   Infants 38
      Diagnosing Infant Injury 42
   Teens and Adults 48

When, Where and Why to Refer Auto Accident Patients

Adults 53
   Whiplash and Soft Tissue Injuries can be Nebulous 53

Insurance 58
The Winds of Change 63
Insurance Software 65
Personal Injury Protection and Med-Pay Insurance 66
How They Work 66
Understanding Utah PIP 66

Treatment Guidelines 71
Maximum Medical Improvement 71
Treatment Protocols and Guidelines 72
National Institute for Neurological Disorders Guidelines 73
Chiropractic, Physical Medicine and Physical Therapy Guidelines ... 74
The Mercy Guidelines 75
The Quebec Task Force Guidelines 76
   The Croft guidelines categorize the following: 79
Type 80
Stages 82
Grades 83
Complicating Factors 84
   Listed below are some complicating risk factors. 85
Prognosis & Motor Vehicle Collision Occupant Injury Risk Factors: .. 87
Croft Guidelines for Diagnosis and Treatment of Whiplash Injuries .. 92
   Croft Guidelines Pros and Cons 94
   The Croft Guideline Pros: 94
   The Croft Guideline Cons: 94

Physicians 96
First Response 97
Emergency Room 97
Instacare/Urgent Care/After Hours Medical 98
Chiropractic Physicians 98
Physical Therapists 100
Licensed Massage Therapist 101
Orthopedic Surgeon 101
Spine Specialist 101
Psychologist 102
Other Specialist 102
Impairment Ratings/Reports 103
Disability Report 104

Attorneys 105
Personal Injury Attorneys 105
Personal Injury Health Care: 105
   Examination 109
   Causation 111
   Objective Proof 114
   "Malingering" or "Non-Organic" Findings 115

Treatment Protocols 117
Epilogue 122
Research 125

♦ The Personal Injury Conundrum

Frequency and Duration of
Treatment for Whiplash Injuries **147**
    Treatment Recommendation based on Grade: *160*
    References: *161*
Certified Professionals **169**
About the Author **170**
How to Engage the Author **173**
Additional Books in The Conundrum Series: **174**

Introduction

Every physician takes an oath: an oath to honor the health and wellbeing of their patients; an oath to strive for perfection in our individual skill as a doctor; an oath, to offer our best to our patients while remaining humble enough that when we don't know the answers, we choose to work with other colleagues for the betterment of the patient.

The climate of health and trauma care is in a constant state of change, at times improving or even redefining itself. In modern health care, broad or "general" practice is a shrinking field. It is being replaced by "specialty" care.

It is not possible for any one of us physicians to have all the answers. Increasingly, physicians have begun to focus on specialized areas in medicine, health, disease, trauma, and rehabilitative care.

As physicians, we need to be acutely aware of when we have what the patient needs and when we do not so that we can refer them to a physician specializing in the area of that patient's health challenges.

Puncture wounds and gunshot wounds are easy diagnoses, but soft tissue injuries, especially those which occur in less prominent muscle groups and tendons, are a different story. Dr. Shetlin clearly makes the point that auto accidents injuries are much more complex. The physics involved, the hidden soft tissue injuries, the long-term negative effects of a misdiagnosis, under diagnosis, treatment and rehabilitation, have a devastating effect on patients even if they do not initially experience the text-book symptoms we look for.

Auto accident injuries entail issues that we as medical doctors rarely care to deal with. Different insurance systems, litigation issues, neck and back pain, lengthy rehab, long-term care and other factors can complicate treatment.

I have worked with doctors of chiropractic as well as physical therapists for years. I have utilized them in my own practice. The aid their skills offer to patients should not be over looked, especially relating to soft tissue injuries.

All physicians, regardless of our specialty, should understand when we can help and when we should refer. Auto accident injury care is a specialty in itself.

Rachot Vacharothone, MD
After Hours Medical
801-260-1919

The Modern Hippocratic Oath

I swear to fulfill, to the best of my ability and judgment, this covenant:

I will respect the hard-won scientific gains of those physicians in whose steps I walk, and gladly share such knowledge as is mine with those who are to follow.

I will apply, for the benefit of the sick, all measures [that] are required, avoiding those twin traps of overtreatment and therapeutic nihilism.

I will remember that there is art to medicine as well as science, and that warmth, sympathy, and understanding may outweigh the surgeon's knife or the chemist's drug.

I will not be ashamed to say "I know not," nor will I fail to call in my colleagues when the skills of another are needed for a patient's recovery.

I will respect the privacy of my patients, for their problems are not disclosed to me that the world may know. Most especially must I tread with care in matters of life and death. If it is given to me to save a life, all thanks. But it may also be within my power to take a life; this awesome responsibility must be faced with great humbleness and awareness of my own frailty. Above all, I must not play at God.

I will remember that I do not treat a fever chart, a cancerous growth, but a sick human being, whose illness may affect the person's family and economic stability. My responsibility includes these related problems, if I am to care adequately for the sick.

I will prevent disease whenever I can, for prevention is preferable to cure.

I will remember that I remain a member of society, with special obligations to all my fellow human beings, those sound of mind and body as well as the infirm.

If I do not violate this oath, may I enjoy life and art, respected while I live and remembered with affection thereafter. May I always act so as to preserve the finest traditions of my calling and may I long experience the joy of healing those who seek my help.

This modern version of the traditional oath was penned in 1964 by Dr. Louis Lasagna, former principal of the Sackler School of Graduate Biomedical Sciences and Academic Dean of the School of Medicine at Tufts University.

Glossary of Terms, Abbreviations, and Symbols

Δ: The delta symbol, meaning change

ΔV: Change in velocity

Acceleration: Change in velocity over time

Bullet Vehicle: The vehicle in motion striking a secondary object or vehicle.

Crumple Zone: Area of the car that is designed to collapse in a high energy collision

Force: Size and weight of an object multiplied by the acceleration

g's or *g-force*: a standard unit of acceleration or deceleration

High Speed or High Energy Collision: Collisions where the speed is above ten miles per hour

Impact Vectors: Magnitude and direction of force of impact during an automobile accident

Impulse: Force applied over time

Inertia: An objects resistance to change in movement

Kinetic Energy: Energy caused by the motion of an object

Low Speed or Low Energy Collisions: Collisions where the speed is at or below ten miles per hour

MVC: Motor Vehicle Collision

Momentum: Mass times velocity

Target Vehicle: The vehicle being struck

Vectors: Magnitude and direction of a force

Velocity: Distance over a period of time

Brief History of Automobile Development and Injuries

Early automobiles were a beauty to behold. The ingenuity alone would leave an onlooker awe-struck. They presented a miraculous leap from the horse and buggy to engine and body.

As automotive innovators improved on these early design, creating cars that were sleeker and more powerful, they also created a plethora of new possibilities for physical injuries, injuries that our own physical evolution was not prepared to prevent.

Initially, automobile manufacturers placed little emphasis on safety; instead they focused on speed, strength and shine. In the 1950s, cars looked stylish but were also incredibly strong. Like a chrome-plated tank, most cars could be crashed into a tree or barrier with little damage to the vehicle itself. In the event of an accident, the vehicle would be towed, scratches buffed out of the chrome plated bumper and voila! The outside would look nearly new.

The interior, however, was a different story. Occupants typically were horribly maimed or killed by the force transferred to their body through the vehicle. (See the detailed discussion in "Motor Vehicle Collision Physics 101" on page 9.) Imagine a young high school couple on their date to the prom. The son borrows his dad's 1957 Chevy. As he shows off the car's power, he doesn't realize how fast he is coming up on a sharp corner. While making oogly eyes at his beautiful date, he zigs when he should have slowed for a zag. Suddenly, the vehicle is out of control and hits a tree.

The interior has upholstered seats, but everything else on the inside is painted steel or polished chrome—zero protection for these two young individuals as the forces of this 3000 lb Chevy come to an abrupt stop against a tree. With his hands braced on the steering wheel, as often times would happen, the wheel itself breaks and the steel shaft impales the driver through the chest. Meanwhile, his passenger crushes her face on the shiny-edged steel dashboard—that is if she doesn't go right through the windshield.

This sort of scenario was not uncommon in the earlier days of automobile development. Manufacturers had not taken into account the higher risk associated with higher speeds; however, with severe injury and deaths on the rise, they began researching ways to improve automobile safety. At the same time, automobile insurance carriers began influencing governments to increase regulations while motivating car manufactures to obtain higher safely ratings, leading to improvements in safety that have included seatbelts, airbags, crumple zones, and other changes that benefit vehicle drivers and passengers.

Evolution Toward Seatbelts and Airbags

Seatbelts

In the 1930s plastic surgeon Claire L. Straith and physician C.J. Strickland advocated the use of seatbelts and padded dashboards.[1] Unfortunately, it took years before these suggestions were taken seriously.

Once implemented, the use of lap seatbelts along with padded dashboards provided only limited assistance in reducing injuries to vehicle occupants. While lap seatbelts did offer assistance in keeping passengers from being ejected from a vehicle during a collision— they may have even helped reduce the number of steering column impalements—the quarter-inch padding on a dashboard simply did

---

1. http://en.wikipedia.org/wiki/Automobile_safety

not provide enough protection to reduce the **rapid change in velocity**. Therefore, front seat drivers and passengers continued to damage their heads, faces and/or teeth on steering wheels and dashboards.

Three-Point Lap and Shoulder Seatbelts

In 1959, Volvo engineer Nils Bohlin invented and patented the three-point lap and shoulder seatbelt, but it took decades before they became mandatory in all vehicles. Even when seatbelts became a requirement for manufacturers, many drivers and passengers would not use these safety devices until laws required it. The three-point harness has proven to be very helpful (when used) in preventing occupants from being ejected from the vehicle and decreasing the number of steering wheel, dash, and windshield impact injuries. *They do, however, increase the frequency of whiplash and hidden soft tissue injuries related to the spine and nervous system.*[2] *This includes low-speed collisions.*

In 1984, New York State passed the first US law requiring seatbelt use in passenger cars. Now all 50 states have adopted similar laws. It is estimated that seatbelts save 10,000 lives per year in the USA.

Safety Testing and Airbags

In 1979 the National Highway Traffic Safety Administration began crash-testing popular cars and publishing the results to inform consumers about the safety of a given vehicle. Public access to safety information encouraged manufacturers to improve the safety of their vehicles.

Most of these tests involved crash test dummies.

In 1995, the Insurance Institute for Highway Safety (IIHS) began conducting frontal offset crash tests.[3]

In 2003 the IIHS began conducting side impact crash tests. Soon researchers were measuring the "change of velocity" and "*g-forces*" applied to crash test dummies and actually began quantitatively measuring the massive amount of energy transmitted through a vehicle to its occupants at the moment of impact.

---

2. Arthur C. Croft, DC, MS, MPH

3. http://www.crashtest.com/explanations/iihs/index.htm

1999 to 2004 additional crash research was performed by Dr. Croft and the Spine Research Institute of San Diego. These collisions included crash test dummies and actual **live occupants** who volunteered to be in controlled crash tests. Most were low-speed collisions, but they varied from rear, side, and frontal impact, with airbag vs. without airbag, male occupant vs. female occupant, and braced vs. unexpected impacts. Additionally, there were some high speed collisions including the first human occupants dual airbag testings. Crash movies have been made available by the Spinal Research Institute of San Diego and testing results are fascinating.

Through these tests and other reports, it became clear that seatbelts alone were not enough in high-speed collisions to reduce the forces applied to a human body; therefore, research for additional or secondary restraints was in order.

Airbags

Mercedes-Benz engineers had begun working on airbag technology in the 1960s. "We used missile technology," remembers Helmut Patzelt, one of the founding fathers of the airbag and an expert in pyrotechnics. "A missile receives its thrust from discharged gas, and we applied this very principle. The only difference is that we trapped the gas—in an airbag."

Rudimentary patents for airbags go back to the 1950s. Patent applications were submitted by German Walter Linderer and American John Hedrik as early as 1951. Unfortunately, the technology to develop such a device and the legal pressure to require airbags in cars would not come for decades.

In 1971, the Ford car company built an experimental airbag fleet. General Motors tested airbags on the 1973 model Chevrolet automobiles that were only sold for government use. The 1973 Oldsmobile Toronado was the first car intended for sale to the public that included a passenger airbag. General Motors later offered an option of driver side airbags in full-sized Oldsmobile's and Buick's in 1975 and 1976 respectively. Cadillacs were available with driver and passenger airbag options during those same years. Early airbag systems had design issues resulting in fatalities caused solely by the airbags.[4]

---

4. http://inventors.about.com/od/astartinventions/a/air_bags.htm

Airbags were offered once again as an option on the 1984 Ford Tempo automobile. By 1988, Chrysler became the first US company to offer airbag restraint systems as standard equipment. In 1994, TRW Automotive began production of the first gas-inflated airbag. Their popularity as a *secondary restrain system* grew quickly. Airbags have been mandatory in most automobiles since 1998.

Airbag Safety

With the advent of airbags, seatbelts took on another role. Airbags are designed to reduce the occupants' *change of velocity* and the *g-forces* applied to the human body when individuals are involved in "high-speed" collisions. Airbags should not deploy in *low energy* collisions (defined as an impact less than 10 miles per hour delta V). When a vehicle experiences a high speed collision, airbags may activate. Early model frontal airbags exploded at 3000 lbs per square inch with a velocity of 295 miles per hour—directly toward the occupant's face. Newer airbags deploy around 2500 lbs. per square inch. Because of this, the three-point seatbelt now has an added job of keeping occupants out of the "explosion zone" of the airbag.

Originally airbags were designed to be mounted on the shoulder harness portion of the seatbelt so that they could explode away from the occupants. From a physician's perspective, this is the more logical design. However, because it is one dollar cheaper to mount them in the steering column and dashboard where they explode toward the occupants, manufacturers chose the second option. Because airbags in their current position explode towards the occupant, when traveling in a vehicle equipped with airbags, there are three important safety points to remember.

- Seatbelts must be used in order for the airbag to function properly. Without the seatbelt, the occupant will most likely end up in the explosion zone before the airbag deploys. In this scenario the airbag becomes a health-hazard rather than a protection device.
- Both driver and passenger must meet the height and weight requirements to be in proper position for these safety features. Drivers and passengers who do not meet these requirements are at risk of injury because they have a higher risk of ending up in the "explosion zone."

- Driver and passenger who meet the requirements must still remain in the proper position. When a driver or front passenger is out of position at the time of impact the seatbelt cannot keep the individual out of the airbag explosion zone. In other words, leaning forward to adjust the radio, bending forward to pick up something off the floor, or putting feet up on the dashboard can all lead to improper positioning which may result in serious injury or death.

Brief History of Treatment Guidelines

This will be addressed in detail later but understand that in 1993, the Croft Guidelines for rehabilitation of cervical acceleration/deceleration injuries (whiplash) were published. These guidelines continue to provide doctors with a research-based road map for helping motor vehicle collision occupant injuries; whiplash victims maximize their healing recovery potential following trauma through proper care. Automobile insurance companies do not readily address or support this patient care standard. Other than their usual cutting of patient bills with other means they do not deal with this system—that is until a case goes to litigation.

Due to increasing cost to automobile insurance companies related to MVCs occupant injuries, the insurance industry regularly looks for ways to save expenses by limiting medical care.

In 1993, the Guidelines for Chiropractic Quality Assurance and Practice Parameters—more commonly known as the Mercy Guidelines—were developed by a 35-member commission initially sponsored by the Congress of Chiropractic State Associations (COCSA). These Mercy guidelines were developed in a closed session by 35 panel members without input from the health care profession at large. No explanation was given as to how these 35 individuals were selected.

Regrettably, these guidelines lacked clarity for diagnosing the severity of injuries, categorizing injuries, and treating injuries. Instead, they were rushed into the hands of insurance companies to set a "standard of care" for the medical/chiropractic treatment of patients following a MVC. Sadly, the Mercy Guidelines became the weighted standard for years, attempting to force doctors to limit their care in the proper rehabilitation.

In Canada, the Quebec Automobile Insurance Society funded a group called the "Quebec Task Force" whose job was to come up with a diagnosis and treatment protocol for whiplash or whiplash associated disorders (WAD). Though the organization made some good points, its driving factor was not maximizing patient recovery, but reducing insurance company losses by paying as little as possible for patient work loss.

In 2000, the Mercy guidelines were found to be nearly useless for physicians in regards to MVC injuries and soft tissue injury rehabilitation.[5]

In addition, the Mercy document had been ruled inadmissible as evidence for testimony on a soft tissue injury.[6]

Currently, the USA averages **1.5 million** MVCs per year.

There are approximately **3 million whiplash** injuries due to MVCs per year. **Approximately 50% of crashed occupants end up with chronic symptoms or pain.** 10% are left disabled.[7] Chronic conditions may be avoided or reduced by proper cervical acceleration/deceleration (CAD) diagnosis and early/appropriate treatment[8] as recommended

---

5. The Mercy document was to be updated and revised. It has never been updated and, in June 2000, the California Chiropractic Association, which had contributed to the conference and was one of the few organizations to give the guidelines a provisional endorsement, passed a resolution ending its support, saying the document "no longer represents the present state of scientific evidence." http://www.worldchiropracticalliance.org/Positions/mercy.htm The Chiropractic profession seems to have forged a specialty "niche" for soft-tissue injuries and has certification courses for MVC injury diagnosis and treatment. Nearly every Chiropractic organization on both the national level and state organizations have rejected the Mercy document related to guidelines for treatment or care of injuries following a motor vehicle injury.

6. (Reeves vs. Flaherty, et al. Expert testimony by Robert Martines, D.C., Santa Clara Superior Court, March 1999; citation: Case # CV758647 Santa Clara County Eva Sue Reeves VS. David Flaherty)

7. Arthur C. Croft, DC, MS, MPH

8. Emil Seletz, MD, a prominent neurosurgeon from Beverly Hills, CA and associated with the medical school at the University of California, Los Angeles (UCLA) published an article in 1958 in the Journal of the American Medical Association in which he emphasized that, 1- "Treatment of whiplash injuries must be started early and must be persistently administered by those expertly trained in physical therapy and rehabilitation." 2 - Care should be carried out daily during the first two or three weeks (and then about three times weekly) depending, of course, on the

by the Croft Guidelines. Interdisciplinary care is often warranted in MVC occupant injury cases, but until insurance companies recognize the importance of covering proper care for these injuries, many accident victims will not seek the proper care they need, which can lead to more expensive, chronic conditions later on in life.

individual case." [Summary by Dr. Dan Murphy]

Motor Vehicle Collision Physics 101

If you have not had a physics class, don't worry. This chapter is not intimidating. It does offer some basic physics vocabulary to learn and reference as it applies to vehicles and human occupants. Familiarize yourself with these terms, then we will get into easy ways to understand and apply the physics of a motor vehicle collision (MVC) to human anatomy. The Insurance Institute for Highway Safety offers a great video teaching some of these scientific principles.

> **The Insurance Institute for Highway Safety offers a great video teaching some of these scientific principles. It is available at www.iihs.org/videos/default.html.**
>
> Some crash videos are also available for viewing at shetlin.com.
>
> A FREE membership password is required to view the material. For questions, contact (801) 446-5100.

Many of these terms are included in the glossary at the beginning of this book, but this chapter includes more elaborate definitions and examples. Pay particular attention to inertia, change of velocity, impulse and *g's* or *g-force*.

Inertia

Newton's First Law of Motion—Simply put, this is an object's resistance to change. If an object is sitting still, it resists movement in any direction without force applied to it. It is inertia that allows the plates to stay on a table when the table cloth is quickly pulled out from under it.

When an occupant is in a vehicle moving at 25 miles per hour from inside the vehicle, it is as if the occupant is not moving. Observing from outside it appears both the vehicle and occupant are moving together at the same 25 miles per hour. Once an object is in motion, it takes a force large enough to overcome this inertia to make it slow, stop, or change direction.

Change of Velocity

If we are driving 10 miles per hour and hit a telephone pole, which brings us to a sudden and abrupt stop (0 miles per hour) our change in velocity (represented in the physics world by delta or the triangle "Δ" followed by a V for velocity) is 10 mph ΔV. If we are stopped at a light (moving at 0 mph) and are rear-ended by a moving vehicle, our car is forced forward from 0 mph to suddenly moving at 6 mph. Our ΔV has instantly changed to 6 mph ΔV. Change of Velocity, as it applies to human anatomy and injury, is a key component that will be addressed in this chapter.

LEGEND
t = time
F = force or (mass) x (acceleration)
a = acceleration
m = mass
Δ = change
v = velocity
K = kinetic
E = energy

Acceleration

$$a = \frac{\Delta v}{t}$$

Acceleration is your change of velocity over a period of time.[9] If we are stopped at a traffic light, we have a velocity of 0 miles per hour. When the light changes and we step on the gas pedal, the vehicle begins moving forward. If it takes us 10 seconds to reach 25 miles per hour then our acceleration is 25mph/10: equaling 2.5.

Force

Force equals the size and weight of an object multiplied by the acceleration. Where force is represented by a capital F, mass represented by a small m, and acceleration represented by a small a, the equation would look like this: F=ma.

$$F = ma$$

$$F = \frac{m\Delta v}{t}$$

Speaking of vehicles, if we have a semi-truck weighing 80,000 lbs. and a Volkswagen Bug weighing 3000 lbs., and they are both traveling at 10

---

9. t=time, F=force or (mass) x (acceleration), P=momentum or (mass) x (velocity), a=acceleration, m=mass, Δ=change, v=velocity, K=kinetic, E=energy

miles per hour, the semi-truck will have more force. Their acceleration is the same, but their mass is vastly different. The same acceleration multiplied by more mass equals greater force.

If that same semi-truck were travelling 1 mph, and that same Volkswagen Bug were travelling at 100 mph, then the Volkswagen Bug would actually have more force than the semi-truck.

Energy

Energy comes in many forms, but in this chapter, we will deal specifically with kinetic energy: energy caused by motion. When an object of any mass is in motion, it will create a measureable amount of energy. Kinetic energy is one half of the mass times the velocity squared: ½ mv 2. Because of this exponential relationship, when we double the speed, we quadruple the kinetic energy.

$$KE = \frac{1}{2}mv^2$$

Momentum

Momentum relates to both mass and velocity. When a mass is in motion at a certain velocity, we figure the momentum by multiplying the mass by that velocity. In physics, momentum is represented by the letter P. So the equation we use to figure momentum is written P=mv.

Impulse

$$P = mv$$

This is vitally important. Impulse equals force applied over time. Rapid impulse or a change of velocity too quickly can cause disaster in any situation, but especially in an MVC.

When there is a large force applied over a short period of time, injury is often the result. A small force applied over a long period of time (Δt) should result in less chance of injury.

To better illustrate the difference between low and high impulse, I've provided a few examples.

- Being pushed in a fight vs. being punched in a fight illustrates this difference. The push is a smaller force applied over a longer period of time, thus it generally results in less injury to soft tissue.
- In a motor vehicle, the difference between gradually applying the brakes to stop a vehicle vs. ramming a telephone pole, thus stopping a vehicle shows the stark contrast between low impulse and high impulse.

Throwing an egg at a wall vs. throwing an egg at a draped sheet is also an effective example. As illustrated below, the high impulse collision between the egg and the wall results in a broken egg, whereas the low impulse collision between the egg and the sheet will usually leave the egg intact.

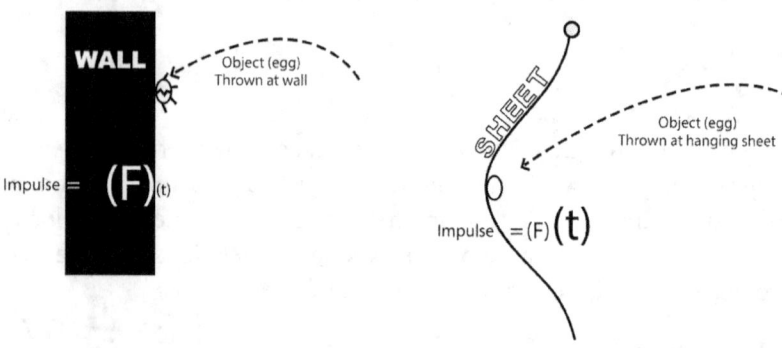

G-force or g's

G-force is not a unit of force but rather a standard unit of acceleration or deceleration.

Human tolerances depend on the magnitude of the *g-force*, the length of time it is applied, the direction it takes, the location of application, and the posture of the body.[10][11]

The human body is flexible and deformable, particularly the softer tissues. A hard slap on the face may briefly impose a high *g-force* locally, but not produce any real or permanent damage; a constant 16 *g* for a minute, however, can be deadly.

The mechanical stress a *g* produces creates energy which may be felt. This is so even if there is no overall coordinant acceleration (as in the example of an object sitting on the ground). As a measurement of acceleration, *g-forces* are considered a *vector quantity*; thus, *g-force* can be negative. A classic example of negative *g* is in a fully inverted roller

---

10. Balldin, Ulf I (2002). "33". Acceleration effects on fighter pilots. In: Medical conditions of Harsh Environments. 2. Washington, DC. http://www.bordeninstitute.army.mil/published_volumes/harshEnv2/harshEnv2.html. Retrieved 2009-04-06.

11. Balldin, Ulf I (2002). "33". Acceleration effects on fighter pilots. In: Medical conditions of Harsh Environments. 2. Washington, DC. http://www.bordeninstitute.army.mil/published_volumes/harshEnv2/harshEnv2.html. Retrieved 2009-04-06.

coaster. In this case, the roller coaster riders are accelerated toward the ground faster than gravity when going over the top of the loop and are pinned upside down in their seats by a net pull in the same direction to gravity. In this case, the mechanical force exerted by the seat causes the *g-force* by altering the path of the passenger. Whether one is accelerating in a free fall, or is acting against gravitational acceleration by standing in one spot on the surface of the earth, or is accelerating or decelerating in any direction, all accelerations, or the lack thereof, are described by Newton's laws of motion.

The Laws of Motion and Motor Vehicle Collisions

The Second Law of Motion, the law of acceleration states that: $F = ma.$, meaning that a force F acting on a body is equal to the **mass** m of the body times its acceleration a.

The Third Law of Motion, the law of reciprocal actions states the following: all forces occur in pairs, and these two forces are equal in magnitude and opposite in direction. Newton's third law of motion not only means that gravity behaves as a force acting downwards on an object, for example, a rock held in your hand, but also that your hand must generate an equal and opposite force upwards if the rock is to remain stationary. If you drop the rock, there are no longer equal forces acting upon the rock, and it will accelerate downwards.

In an airplane, the pilot's seat can be thought of as the hand holding the rock, the pilot as the rock. When flying straight and level at 1 g, the pilot is acted upon by the force of gravity. His weight (a downward force) is 725 newtons (163 lbf). In accordance with Newton's third law, the plane and the seat underneath the pilot provides an equal and opposite force pushing upwards with a force of 725 N (163 lbf). If the pilot were to suddenly pull back on the stick and make his plane accelerate upwards at 9.8 m/s2, the total *g-force* on his body is 2 g. His body is now generating a force of 1,450 N (330 lbf) downwards into his seat and the seat is simultaneously pushing upwards with an equal force of 1,450 N (330 lbf).

Unlike the airplane seat example, an automobile and its driver experience what is called lateral acceleration. Acceleration due to mechanical forces, and consequentially *g-force*, is experienced whenever anyone rides in a vehicle because it is the rate at which speed (velocity) changes. Whenever the vehicle changes either direction or speed, the occupants feel lateral (side to side) or longitudinal (forward and backwards) forces produced by the mechanical push of their seats.

The expression "1 g = 9.80665 m/s2" (or for those not converted to the metric system, it would be approximately, "1 g = 32 feet/s2") means that *for every second* elapsed, velocity changes 9.80665 meters ($\equiv$35.30394 km/h). This rate of change in velocity can also be noted as 9.80665 **per** second, or 9.80665 m/s2. For example, an acceleration of 1 g equates to a rate of change in velocity of approximately 35 kilometers per hour (22 mph) for each second that elapses. Therefore, if an automobile is capable of braking at 1 g and is traveling at 35 kilometers per hour (22 mph), the car can brake to a standstill in one second and the driver will experience a deceleration of 1 g. The automobile traveling at three times this speed, 105 km/h (65 mph) can brake to a standstill in three seconds.

The following may not be the exact physics definition, but it clarifies the meaning as it relates to MVCs and injury: impulse is a change of velocity under force. If the force of a vehicle in motion slows or accelerates faster than the human occupant's tissues can make a healthy adaptation the occupant is injured. Unfortunately, because of this, injury can happen in a motor vehicle collision even if the vehicle is travelling just over 5 miles per hour.

Mass in Motion

Let's apply some physics in layman's terms. Dr. Jeffrey States, a friend and personal injury certification instructor, refers to one rule-of-the-road as the lug-nut rule. Put simply, when two or more vehicles are involved in a MVC the vehicle with the most lug-nuts usually wins because the vehicle with the most lug-nuts will most likely be the vehicle with greater mass. Because of this rule, the potential for occupant injury in the larger vehicle is less than the potential for injury in the smaller vehicle. This does not mean that occupants in a larger/heavy vehicle are not injured; however, the potential for injury is reduced.

Whiplash and Hidden Soft Tissue Injuries

WIN		LOSE
Smart Car (3 lugs/wheel)	VS	Ten Speed Bike (1 lug/wheel)
Honda Accord (5 lugs/wheel)	VS	Motor Cycle (1 lug/wheel)
Typical SUV (6 lugs/wheel)	VS	Smart Car (3 lugs/wheel)
Semi with Trailer (10 lugs/wheel)	VS	Any Car or SUV

While the lug-nut rule does have exceptions because of certain complicating factors, it is still a good rule of thumb in determining which occupants will receive the greater amount of forces applied to their bodies and therefore has greater potential for occupant injuries. The vehicle with the greatest deceleration due to its smaller mass will be the vehicle whose occupants are at greatest risk in a collision.

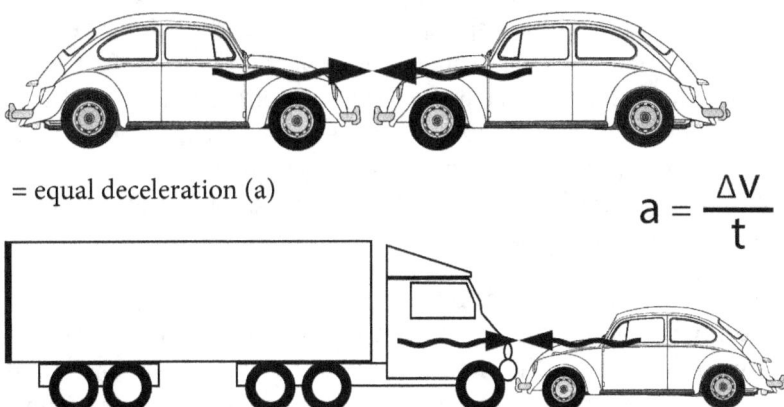

= equal deceleration (a)

$$a = \frac{\Delta V}{t}$$

= increased deceleration (a) for the little car.

Using a head-on collision as an example, two equal-sized vehicles going the same speed have equal deceleration. Whereas in a collision involving one large vehicle and a smaller vehicle, the smaller vehicle will have an increased deceleration thus increasing the likelihood of injury. There you have "The Lug-nut Rule."

Vehicle Mass and Acceleration force

"Acceleration depends on the force applied and the inertia of the vehicle that has been struck. The force is dependent upon the weight and speed of the striking vehicle, so that a streetcar traveling at 3 mph can apply as much force and initiate the same degree of acceleration as a compact car traveling at 40 mph."[12]

This is an important point in the misconception the public has with a "5 star rating" for crash tests. This rating system is testing how a vehicle does in a crash with a fixed object. Understanding Newton's third law where equal and opposite force is applied, this is the equivalent of the vehicle crashing into a vehicle identical to itself. However, as the lug-nut rule makes clear, if a vehicle of greater mass impacts a vehicle of lesser mass, the forces exchanged are greater. Translation, the 5 star rating doesn't mean much in real world crashes with variable sized vehicles.

Low Speed vs. High Speed Collisions

Another essential factor in injury has to do with the speed of the collision. This is probably the most misunderstood variable regarding motor vehicle collisions and occupant injuries. First, we need to clarify the difference between low speed and high speed. Surprisingly, vehicles do not have to be traveling at 50 plus miles per hour for a motor vehicle collision to be considered a high speed collision. In fact, the break off point is just 10 miles per hour. Any collision over 10 miles per hour is considered, and should be documented, as a high speed or high energy collision. Anything less than 10 miles per hour delta V is classified as a low speed or lower energy collision."

A properly prepared police report, or a medical report prepared by a Certified Motor Vehicle Occupant Injuries Professional, [13] should distinguish whether the incident was a high speed or low speed collision. The exact speed of the collision is quite difficult to determine, but providing a reference point of high speed or low speed is relatively simple.

---

12. Ian Macnab, Associate Professor of Surgery, University of Toronto Chief of Division of Orthopedic Surgery, Wellesley Hospital, Toronto."Acceleration Extension Injuries of the Cervical Spine" Chapter 10 in THE SPINE by Rothman and Simeone. WB Saunders Company 1982 Page 648

13. Find the current list of MVCOI Certified Professionals http://personalinjurytraininginstitute.com/certpros.html

One of the mistakes people make, however, is assuming that a low speed collision equates to a reduced chance of injury. Statistically, more people are injured in low speed collisions than in high speed collisions.

This surprising statistic can be attributed to several key factors, all of which have to do with the physics of motor vehicle collisions.

Crumple Zones

As we discussed briefly in the history section, older cars were built like chrome-plated tanks. Their frame work was incredibly strong and rigid. They were able to withstand forceful impacts with minimal body damage. These older cars had such rigidity that the vehicle itself would experience less **deceleration**. This meant the occupants inside the vehicle would experience a greater **deceleration** or **impulse**.

To avoid the often deadly results of rigidly designed vehicles, newer vehicles are now designed with crumple zones which purposefully collapse upon impact. By so doing they allow more time (Δt) over which force (f) can be distributed, thereby reducing the actual deceleration or impulse to the occupants.

By design, crumple zones will engage only during high energy collisions, not lower energy collisions. Cost is a factor in every manufactured product, and it simply would not be cost effective to have them engage in minor collisions. The reason for this is that when crumple zones are activated, there is typically significant damage to the vehicle. Oft times the vehicle is totaled. In the automotive industry it would be wasteful to have every car in the slightest fender-bender to end up as scrap metal. As for the insurance industry, it would be devastating to pay damages related to this many vehicles per year. Thus, there has to be a happy medium. There are two solutions to this dilemma:

- Crumple zones for high-speed collisions. (more vehicle damage hopefully yielding less occupant injury)
- 5 mph bumpers for low-speed collisions. (Less/minimal visible vehicle damage)

As a result, vehicles are engineered such that in a high-speed frontal or rear impact collision, the crumple zone engages to absorb as much force as possible while keeping the "cage" or occupant compartment intact. This crumple zone engineering combined with seatbelts and airbags saves lives in high speed collisions. Even with these technological advances in automotive engineering, thousands of occupants in the US involved in high-speed collisions are killed. Referring back to our statistic of more people being injured in low-speed collisions than high-speed, one reason is those killed in high-speed collisions (and their data) are moved into a different statistical category.

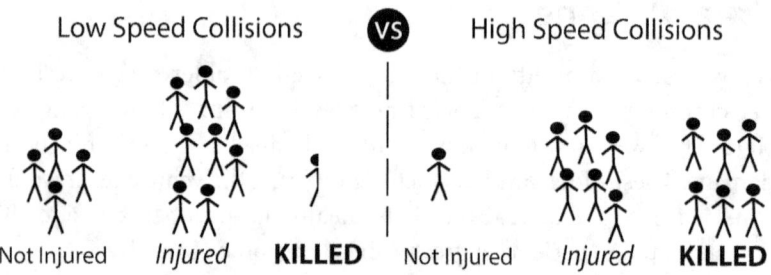

Another factor brings us back to basic physics. If a vehicle is involved in a low-speed collision or in other words, no crumple zone is engaged to help absorb (f) force over (t) time, then where do all the forces go? The answer is pivotal in explaining why people are injured in low-speed collisions.

In a low-speed impact, one might ask what happens with momentum, kinetic energy, and change of velocity, Force =(mass)x(acceleration), g's and impulse?

The laws of physics tell us that no two solid objects can occupy the same space at the same time. If we have a vehicle stopped at a red light that is rear-ended at speeds less than 10 miles per hour, there should be no absorption of force by the crumple zone. We also discussed how many bumpers are designed to hide or minimize property damage thereby reducing expensive repairs. Much like a Newton's cradle, upon impact **ALL the energy and force of the 2000 lb–4000 lb vehicle in motion is actually transferred through the frame of the stopped vehicle directly into the occupants.** If an accident report were properly documented, it would label the vehicle in motion as the "bullet vehicle" and the vehicle which was struck while at a standstill the "target vehicle." The physics of the concept of bullet and target vehicles are explained in the following examples.

Newton's Cradle

This demonstration illustrates how the energy and force of the *bullet vehicle* is transmitted through the frame and mass of both vehicles directly into the occupants of the *target vehicle*.

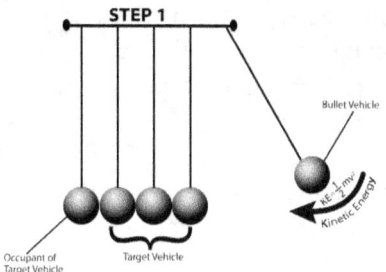

Step 1: Bullet vehicle is moving. Target vehicle and occupant(s) are stopped.

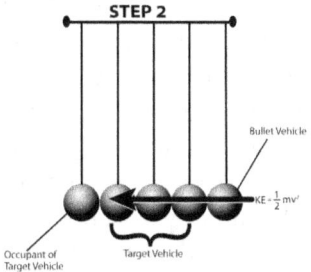

Step 2: Bullet vehicle strikes target vehicle. There is no absorption of force thus the energy is transferred into (or through) the target vehicle.

Step 3: Transfer of energy to the occupant(s) is instant and far greater than typically understood.

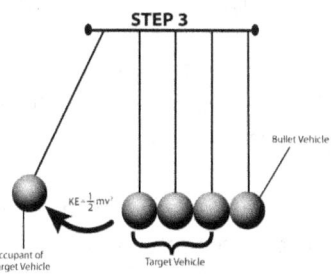

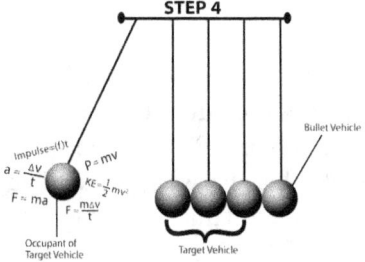

Step 4: Occupant(s) experience a surprisingly intense amount of force and energy with minimal or no visible vehicle damage.

Occupants of both vehicles will experience these forces. However, it is common for the target vehicle occupants of rear-end and side-impact collisions to experience greater injury. Reasons will be discussed in the "complicating factors" section. All of these factors contribute to the misunderstood fact that more people are injured in low-speed collisions than high speed collisions.

In the insurance chapter we will address in more detail how insurance companies typically view low speed collisions. For now, understand that it is standard procedure for an insurance adjuster to inspect a vehicle post MVC. Their job is to decide if it is more cost effective for the company and best for the client to repair the vehicle or simply total the vehicle. Often times they may document something like, "There is minimal damage to the vehicle so it will be better to fix it. Oh, and I doubt anyone was injured."

Records or a comment like this by someone without medical training can be passed on to the head office where the medical adjuster – who surprisingly, also has no medical training – might read it and decide, "Then I don't think we should pay any of the medical bills." This kind of conduct leaves countless individuals struggling from injuries sustained in a low-speed collisions. They find themselves wrestling with their insurance company to get bills paid or worse, not receiving the health care they need early-on, which will lead to greater problems, pain, and accelerated spinal disc disease[14] later in life.

The methods in which data is categorized, combined with engineering to save lives in higher speed collisions while saving property costs in lower speed collisions, are two key reasons why more people are injured in low-speed vs. high-speed motor vehicle collisions. In lower energy collisions the rear-ended or target vehicle becomes a force amplifier increasing energy to the occupants.

Wet or Icy Roads vs. Dry Roads

For those who live in snow and ice climates, this topic needs to be properly addressed. For simplicity sake, let's use a rear-end collision as an example. If we watch the San Diego Spine Research Institute (SRISD) video footage of several rear-end collisions, we see quantified amounts of energy and force equations described in this chapter applied

---

14. Medical Times, November 1921, pp. 1–7 *The Windsor Study*

to human occupants. The institute's footage shows individuals sitting in a *target vehicle* that is then struck from behind by a *bullet vehicle*. The Institute tested various scenarios measuring the ΔV (change of velocity) and the *g's* applied to the occupants. [15] The footage reveals that when the impact is a surprise[16], the individual is not braced; the ΔV and *g's* are greater than when the occupant is able to brace **without locking their arms or joints.**

When watching a rear-end impact with the naked eye, the instantaneous transition of forces are difficult to observe. In slow motion, and with the measuring devices used by the SDSRI, light is shed on common misconceptions.

On dry roads, tires provide traction or friction between the vehicle and the road. With the brakes applied, friction slows/reduces the potential impulse or ΔV of the target vehicle itself, thereby reducing (albeit minimally) some of the ΔV and *g's* transferred to the occupants.

On wet roads, tires provide less traction or friction, thus increasing the ΔV and *g's* the occupants would experience.

Many people think an accident on ice is less intense. It is perceived that cars simply slide away from the point of impact and glide to a gentle stop, unless the vehicle bounces off some other obstacle in its slippery path of motion.

On ice covered roads there is minimal, if any, friction between the target vehicle and the road, thus increasing the impulse or ΔV and *g's* that the occupants will experience. Increased ΔV and *g's* increases the likelihood of injury.

Picture an air hockey table. If the puck is placed in the middle of the table with the air off, there will be friction between the puck and the surface of the table. If the puck is hit with the paddle using "x" amount of force, the puck will travel a minimal distance and come to a stop

---

15. (To see the SDSRI footage visit www.shetlin.com/media. A password is required to view this copy written footage so simply contact Dr. Shetlin's office or Health & Wealth Solutions, LLC by phone or e-mail.)

16. Surprise is defined as the human volunteer occupant does not know the exact moment of impact. They certainly know where they are, what is about to happen especially if there are multiple impacts.

quickly. The puck represents a target vehicle on a dry surface with the brakes applied when struck from behind by a bullet vehicle (the paddle).

If the same table is used with the air on and the puck is hit using the same "x" amount of force, are the results different? Yes! The puck will accelerate away from the impact at a greater rate and will travel much farther. The distance is not necessarily the point of focus but more the *moment of impact*. In the instant the puck (target vehicle) is struck by the paddle (bullet vehicle), due to the reduced friction between the puck and the table, the force, momentum and kinetic energy are directly transferred into the puck with much less, or no, resistance. Thus the ΔV and *g's* are greatly increased. It is the ΔV and *g's* that are critical; when these forces are applied to the body in excess, the result is injury. The same simple impact on ice instead of on a dry road can seriously complicate or exacerbate injury to vehicle occupants.

Research shows that the human body is designed for compressive forces such as running and jogging, but can only withstand shear forces yielding a change of velocity less than 8 mph. Injury can occur with as little as 5 mph ΔV of shear force, but it's practically guaranteed at 8 mph or greater. [17]

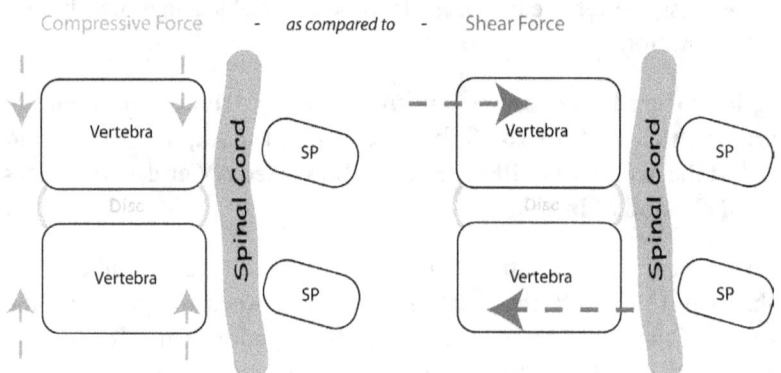

Vehicle Damage vs. Passenger Injury

"The amount of damage sustained by the car bears little relationship to the force applied. To take an extreme example: If the car was stuck in

---

17. Stemper BD, Yoganandan N, Pintar FA, Rao RD. Anterior longitudinal ligament injuries in whiplash may lead to cervical instability. Medical Engineering & Physics 2006;28 512–524

concrete, the damage sustained might be very great but the occupants would not be injured because the car could not move forward, whereas, on ice, the damage to the car could be slight but the injuries sustained might be severe because of the rapid accelerations permitted."[18]

Impact Vectors

There is no question that the vector of travel and impact regarding a MVC dramatically increases or decreases injury potential to occupants. For example, two vehicles hitting with head-on vectors drastically increases the forces applied to the vehicles and occupants. Thus, engineers design crumple zones for frontal and rear impact collisions. A "t-bone" or side impact collision can deliver incredible force directly to occupants. There is minimal engineering available (because there is minimal space to work with) to reduce forces by increasing crash time. The space between the bullet vehicle and occupant is only inches. Yes, there are reinforced doors and now some cars come with side-airbags, but these types of extreme collisions are easily avoidable by simply engineering better roads.

The typical "cross" intersection has enormous accident and injury potential. According to the Arizona Department of Transportation there are 32 potential points of contact/conflict for MVCs. Utahns are a little more creative when it comes to intersection crash vector potentials. According to the Utah driver's handbook there are 57 different conflict points to crash your car. Cross intersections have other downsides, including greatly increased fuel consumption and pollution and, most importantly as pertains to our topic at hand, is the increased injury and fatality.

- 32 points of conflict (57-Utah)
- Increases fuel consumption by double digits!
- Increases injury accidents by 75 percent, and fatal accidents 90 percent

~Arizona DOT

---

18. Ian Macnab, Associate Professor of Surgery, University of Toronto Chief of Division of Orthopedic Surgery, Wellesley Hospital, Toronto.

Many intersections of this nature support traffic stopped in one direction while cross traffic is traveling anywhere from 35 mph up to 75 mph. The simplest mistake making a left-hand turn can be life altering or fatal. *(Figure 1)*

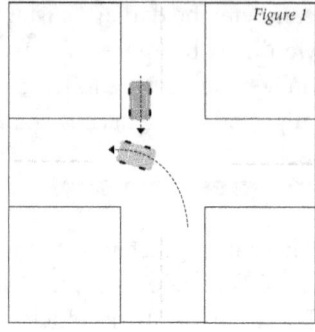
Figure 1

A swerve to avoid debris or a vehicle wandering into your lane can send your vehicle veering into oncoming or perpendicular traffic. *(Figure 2)*

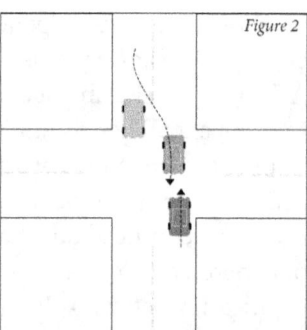
Figure 2

When we study some of the impact vectors in cross intersection and compare them to a roundabout, the data is staggering. Roundabouts have clear advantage to traffic signals in numerous ways, especially regarding safety.

Again quoting the Arizona Department of Transportation, a typical roundabout has only 8 potential points of conflict (Utahns found 14). Roundabouts however, have a variety of shapes and sizes which can affect those numbers.[19] Regardless, there are many advantages to a modern roundabout:

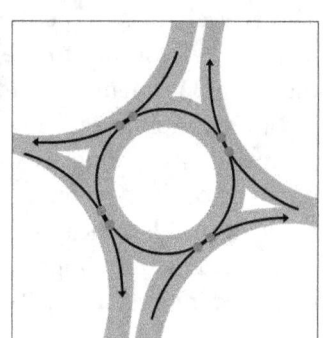

- 8 conflict points (14-Utah)
- Vehicles slow before entering
- Glancing side hits
- Reduces fuel emissions
- Nice piece of art in the center
- Cheap to build
- European cities are often paid bonuses by the state or the European Union to put in roundabout intersections vs. cross intersections.

---

19. US Department of Transportation Federal Highway Administration; Turner-Fairbanks Highway Research Center; McLean, VA; http://www.tfhrc.gov/pubrds/fall95/p95a41.htm

The common modern design requires slowing or yielding to enter the roundabout which in itself reduces the chance of serious injury or fatality. An approaching vehicle simply slows, checks traffic, especially to the left, then makes a right turn to enter the roundabout. Once the desired exit point is reached a right turn is again performed, thus exiting the intersection. Regardless of north, south, east or west, you make a right-turn in and a right-turn out. Roundabouts completely void the need for deadly left-hand turns in an intersection.

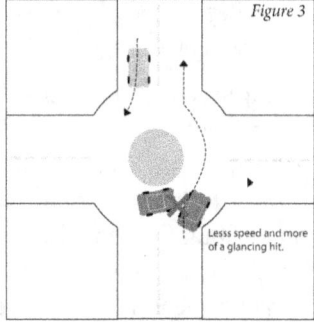

Figure 3

Lesss speed and more of a glancing hit.

If there is a collision, it will be a slower (not necessarily low-speed) impact and, most likely, a glancing hit as compared to a cross intersection. *(Figure 3)* Rear impact collisions are still a strong possibility though they would not have the same ΔV and g's as someone stopped at a cross intersection being struck at 35 mph, or greater, from behind.

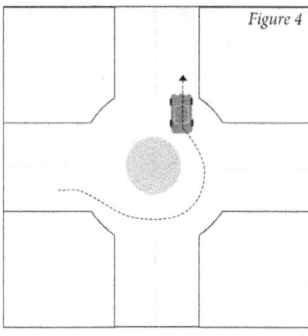

Figure 4

Considering the benefits,

- No left-hand turns where a vehicle has to cross head on traffic. *(Figure 4)*
- No head-on collisions (unless someone is foolish enough to turn left into the roundabout). *(Figure 5)*
- No "t-bone" side-impact collisions.

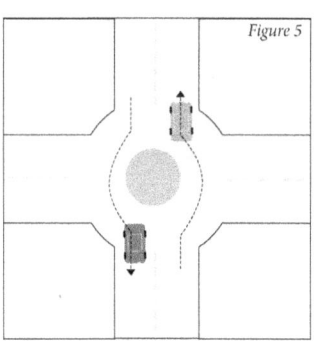

Figure 5

roundabouts are far safer and more cost effective as compared to cross intersections. And, there are additional perks:

- Roundabouts don't require as much stop and go traffic, thus saving on fuel and fuel emissions.
- Roundabouts are inexpensive to build and maintain. There are roundabouts that use lights but most require only signage such as a yield sign and some pretty landscape.

- They can beautify the city or town with art: a statue or a fountain in the center.

Having lived and practiced in both the US and Europe, I have seen firsthand the accidents and injuries from roundabouts are much less severe. As US highway engineers study and acknowledge the data from roundabouts in the US, many of these same engineers are becoming advocates for roundabouts.[20] Though simple in structure and less expensive to build, roundabouts can require some adaptation on our part. The adjustment is a small tradeoff for the reduction in injuries to the next generation and future generations of drivers. For both safety and cost reduction (taxes, insurance, fuel consumption, etc.) we need to move forward with mass implementation of roundabouts across the country.

---

20. US Department of Transportation Federal Highway Administration; Turner-Fairbanks Highway Research Center; McLean, VA; http://www.tfhrc.gov/pubrds/fall95/p95a41.htm

Motor Vehicle Collision Occupant Injuries Anatomy and Physiology

Infant Anatomy

To understand the full potential of the type of injuries sustained from motor vehicle collisions, we have to return to the beginning.

Two cells met (a sperm and an egg) and merged to form a single functional cell known as an embryo. The embryo splits in two, then four, then eight to later become the trillions of cells that make up a human body at birth.

Examine what happens on day 11. Up until day 11 the embryo is simply a ball of identity-neutral cells or stem cells. These cells do not have a specific shape or function just yet. On day 11, however, one of many human miracles takes place. These cells begin to group together forming identities. Humans are "groupies" by nature, even down to this cellular level. Some neighboring cells form into kidney cells, other become eyeball cells, and so on. In this miraculous event a rudimentary version of the nervous system is formed. It is called the *primitive streak*. Thus, the nervous system is the FIRST

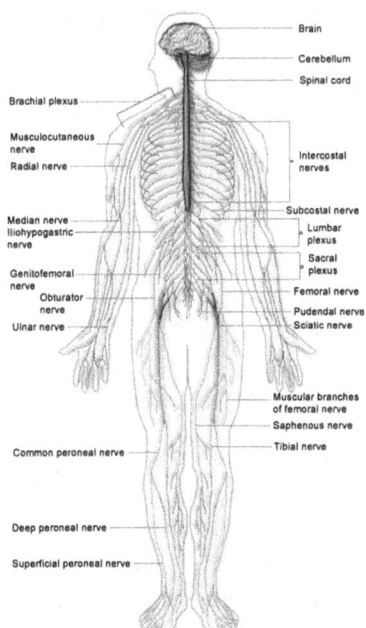

system to develop in the body, and it immediately connects to all the living cells controlling and coordinating growth, development, function and healing from day 11 forward. The nervous system consists of the brain, spinal column and peripheral nerves. Together they form the "central computer" that controls and coordinates the body as a whole.

As an infant's body continues to grow, bones (cartilaginous, at first) form around the central portion of the nervous system as protection. These are the beginning of the spinal vertebrae. Vertebral discs develop between spinal bones to act as spacers and later, in the weight-bearing years, to assist in shock absorption against gravity. While still in utero, other skeletal bones also take shape. Muscles, ligaments, tendons, organs, arteries, veins, skin, fingernails and so on, all form under the control of a single gelatinous mass of neurons called the nervous system.

At birth, the human tissue proportion is far different from that of an adult. In regards to a human adult, the head is approximately one-tenth of the over-all proportionate composition. A newborn is approximately **one-third** head and two-thirds torso and limbs. This can be a complicating factor in dealing with infants and children involved in motor vehicle accidents.

When a baby makes it to full-term, and if the birth process is non-traumatic, the organs, glands and tissues are ready for survival (with nutritional assistance from mom, of course). Bones and nerves have completed the necessary development to protect and run vital organs for breathing, digesting and excreting. The fragile brain and nervous system are surrounded by fluid for protection and suspended by a strong system of tissues called meninges. Muscles and ligaments are present in their proper locations. However, in the case of a baby, it will take months to years for the muscles to develop their strength and coordination. This is another complicating factor regarding infants and children particularly when they are occupants involved in MVCs.

Adult Anatomy

Humans have 22 cranial bones, seven cervical (neck) bones, 12 thoracic (mid back) bones, five lumbar (low back) bones and three to seven pelvic bones depending on the age of the individual. (The five sacrum bones fuse into one in the teen years.) The remaining skeletal bones make up a rough count of 206 bones in the body.

Ligaments attach bones together and act as anchors, limiting the range or amount of movement between the adjacent bones to which they are attached. In the spine, these ligaments are of vital importance because too much (or too little) movement between spinal bones can result in unwanted harmful effects on the delicate nervous system.

Ligaments commonly injured in MVCs include: the alar and transverse ligaments,[21] [22] ligamentum flavum, anterior longitudinal ligament, posterior longitudinal ligament, interspinous ligament and capsular ligament,[23] sacroiliac ligaments and hip stabilization ligaments. Intervertebral disc injury is also possible.

There are approximately 640 skeletal **muscles** in the human body, or 320 pairs of muscles. These tissues attach to the bones via tendons. Muscles can only 'pull,' thus each muscle and tendon is positioned and connected in a way to make movement, or stabilize via tone or contraction.

Spinal muscles are quite susceptible to injury and strain from MVCs. Neck muscles are at an extreme disadvantage. The typical adult human head weighs between 10 and 13 pounds. The forces transferred through a vehicle into the body during a MVC are simply a recipe for disaster. As the head and torso are rapidly moved in opposing directions it creates a whip-like motion yielding tremendous strain on the tiny muscles and ligaments of the neck. Studies have shown how even in a low speed collision the human head can momentarily weigh upwards of 130 lbs leaving one's neck muscles and ligaments at the mercy of physics.

Commonly injured muscles may include: rectus capitis (minor and major), obliquus capitus (superior and inferior), rotator cervicis muscles, semispinalis capitis, splenius capitis, spinalis cervicis, longissimus capitis, scalenes, levator scapulae, sternoclydomastoid,

---

21. Kaale Br, Krakenes J, Albrektsen G, Wester K. Head position and impact direction in whiplash injuries: associations with MRI-verified lesions of ligaments and membranes in the upper cervical spine. Journal of Neurotrauma 2005; 22(11):1294-1302

22. Krakenes J, Kaale BR, Nordi H, Moen G, Rorvik J, Gilhus NE. MRI analysis of the transverse Ligament in the late stage of whiplash injury. Acta Radiologica 2003; 44:637-644

23. Tominaga Y, Ndu AB, Coe MP, et al. Neck ligament strength is decreased following whiplash trauma. BMC Musculoskeletal Disorders 2006; 7:103.

sternothyroid, platysma, pectoralis major, pectoralis minor, deltoids, bicep at origin, tricep at origin, teres (major and minor), subscapularis, quadradus erector spinae group, and hip external/internal flexor group – typically from foot on brake pedal.

Damaged ligaments and muscles will cause a combination of instability (hypermobility) along with muscle guarding (hypertonicity). The result is local inflammation which causes pain; instability which causes pain; muscle spasm with lactic acid build-up which causes pain and decreased mobility at one level with hypermobility at adjacent levels which will lead to long-term problems of degenerative arthritis.

Diagnostic Tools

Static X-ray Film

Diagnosing ligament and muscle injuries from images done with static X-ray film is much more difficult than diagnosing bone injuries. Soft tissues are nearly invisible by standard diagnostic imaging techniques while osseous structures, or bones, are clearly visible on static X-ray.

In order to diagnose ligament and muscle injuries, physicians require other imaging techniques. Physicians certified in the diagnosis and treatment of *CAD injuries* can utilize flexion and extension cervical films using the Penning and AMA guidelines to measure and qualify soft tissue injuries. Penning and AMA measurements are important because they are the guidelines given by the medical association offering physicians a guide of normal vs. abnormal. They are also the most cost-effective first step using imaging to support a diagnosis of soft tissue injury. These measurement techniques are available to all physicians and radiologists, yet they are drastically under-utilized.

Digital Motion X-ray

The next most cost-effective and the most accurate diagnostic imaging tool for ligament injury to date is digital motion X-ray. With motion X-ray, the physician can observe the functional capacity of the ligaments in the neck and extremities with minimal radiation exposure.

Digital motion X-ray utilizes X-ray technology and couples it with new digital and optic technology in the image intensifier to create high-resolution images of the spine and skeletal system in real-time motion.

(DMX can produce 2700 still X-rays with the same radiation dose as the seven (7) view Cervical Davis series.[24])

Presently, motion X-ray is not helpful in thicker body regions such as mid back and low back due to poor image quality. That may change in years to come. Regardless, the technology is currently extremely helpful in thinner body parts. With motion X-ray, joint dysfunction becomes quite clear to even an untrained eye. Damage to the alar ligament, transverse, capsular ligament, interspinous ligament, anterior longitudinal, and posterior longitudinal ligaments will reveal abnormal and excessive movement of the osseous structures. Motion X-ray images are especially helpful because they are taken with the patient *weight bearing*: standing under gravity moving through their own natural ranges of motion. In litigation, even a lay jury member can clearly see areas that are not functioning within normal expected parameters. It is no surprise that many insurance companies fight or resist payment for these images.

MRI

MRI is currently the gold-standard for soft tissue imaging, particularly for disc involvement such as disc derangement, bulging, rupture or fragmentation. It is also helpful for detecting tumors, blood clots or hemorrhaging. MRI imaging is a costly procedure, but it provides valuable detail in visualizing soft tissues. Sadly, MRI is currently a motionless image. This is the downside of MRI; the patients are not in a natural position nor are they truly weight bearing. Artificial loading bearing techniques are available to help simulate weight bearing and create an image with spinal discs under pressure. These have proven to reveal disc injuries that might have been missed on a normal MRI. Motion MRI would be a powerful imaging tool, but is currently unavailable. Some have tried to simulate a motion MRI by changing the position of the patient and retaking an image. Currently the MRI equipment does not allow for true or natural movement since the patient is lying down in a confined tubular space. Only a handful of upright MRI units are available throughout the world. As technology changes upright MRI might become more accessible. Though weight bearing gives more accurate findings it is still not as helpful as a motion image in detecting ligament injury.

---

24. Understanding dynamic motion X-ray/fluoroscopy procedures, findings and medical necessity. http://www.whiplashpro.com/linked/dmx_internet_synopsis.pdf.

Physical Examination

Imaging alone is not enough for complete diagnosis and treatment. It is also insufficient to win a legal case. A detailed examination by a trained physician with appropriate documentation from the history, exam and imaging is the first step in the accurate diagnosis and treatment of injuries sustained from a motor vehicle collision.

Important Factors in Treatment

Blood Vasculature

We don't want to overlook the blood vasculature and potential injury of these tissues related to a motor vehicle injury. If the patient is not visibly bleeding or showing signs of experiencing cognitive dysfunction it is often assumed that the blood vasculature was unharmed. In a whiplash it is important to note two things:

- The neck was flexed and possibly extended beyond its normal ranges under incredible forces in just a fraction of a second. Looking at the diagrams of the head and neck vasculature you can see that if other tissues were moved beyond their normal ranges or damaged, there is possibility the vasculature may have been stretched beyond their limits. The higher in the neck we look the more concerning this becomes. Regardless of whether the head impacts an object such as the head restraint or otherwise, the rapid change of velocity could cause microscopic or larger tears in neck and intracranial vasculature;

- Symptoms may or may not show up right away. This is a particular caution for infants.

Inflammation and Scar Tissue

Although some details of inflammation may vary according to the injury site, most inflammatory responses are quite similar.

Acute inflammation gradually leads to the formation of granulation tissue. This is characterized by the replacement of polymorphonuclear leukocytes by monocytes, lymphociytes, and plasma cells and later by the proliferation of endothelial cells and fibroblasts in the area of injury. Ultimately, these lead to the restoration of the vascular supply and connective tissue matrix, respectively, during the process of repair that normally follow. Under conditions in which the acute inflammatory response fails to come to a successful resolution, however, chronic inflammation develops.

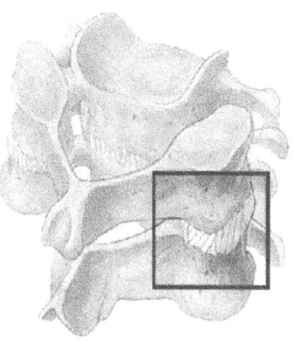

The repair phase of healing ideally results in the restoration of normal living tissue. The successful outcome depends on the interplay of repair by connective tissue replacement and the growth and differentiation of cells in the injured tissue.[25] The repair process is characterized by a high level of activity of fibroblasts, which synthesize matrix components and eventually produce a fibrous scar.

During the remodeling and maturation phase, which usually overlaps repair, the newly accumulated matrix components undergo organizational and orientation changes designed to optimize the structural and functional integrity of the healing tissue. The most striking feature of this process is the laying down of new collagen by activated fibroblasts, about 6 days after lesion.[26] This immature collagen (procollagen) is gel-like, and a process of maturation is required involving cross-linking of collagen molecules into microfibrils and subsequently into fibrils. Initially collagen is laid down randomly. However, during remodeling continuous enzymatic destruction, new synthesis, and reforming of collagen occur, resulting in a more orderly orientation of fibers under the influence of appropriate mechanical loading.[27] Mechanically, the hallmark of the remodeling phase is the reorientation of collagen fibers to lines of wound stress accompanied by a marked increase in wound strength. Under experimental conditions, immobilization of healing wounds has been shown to compromise wound strength, presumably as a result of a failure of collagen fiber orientation along appropriate stress lines.[28] Conversely, mobilization

---

25. Kumar V Coltran RS, Robbins SL. Basic Pathology 6th ed. Phyadelphia: W.B. Saunders;1997

26. Adults and Children. 2nd ed. St. Louis, MO: Mosby; 1994: 234–267

27. McGaw WT. The effect of tension on collagen remodeling by fibroblasts: a stereological ultrastructural study. Connect Tissue Res.1986; 14:229–235

28. Noyes FR, Torvik YJ, Hyde WB, et al. Biomechanics of ligament failure, II: an analysis of immobilization exercise and reconditioning effects in primates. J Bone

with loading has been shown to result in stronger healed tissue.[29] This is extremely important information because it directly impacts how physicians treat collision injuries.

Time Frame of Healing

The acute inflammatory phase is brief and leads to the proliferative-synthetic phase 3–7 days after injury. During the remodeling phase the turnover of collagen may last several months, and maturation may not be complete for **12 months or more after an injury**. Ultimately the nature of the repaired tissue depends on the interaction of many factors, including the age of the patient, the type of tissue, the extent of injury, the site and size of the scar, and forces acting on the scar during the healing process.[30] Skeletal muscle has considerable regenerative capabilities. This is due to their cellular make-up and good blood supply. Tendon injuries including strain (tear), respond quickly. Generally inflammation will occur during the first few days after injury, fibroblastic and vascular contribution may come from various tissues surrounding the injury site.[31] Type III collagen, which has the ability to cross-link rapidly, is the predominant collagen in the initial phase of healing. However, it is gradually replaced by Type I collagen, the major component of the normal extracellular matrix.

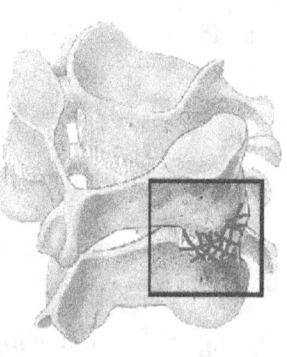

During the proliferative (repair) phase, there is random accumulation of collagen. This continues for about 8 weeks and is followed by a phase of remodeling and maturation, during which collagen fibers become

---

Joint surg Am. 1974;36:1406–1418

29. Exercise and reconditioning effects in primates. J Bone Joint surg Am. 1974;36:1406–1418 Karpakka J, Vaananen K, Virtanen P, et al. The effects of remobilization and exercise on collagen biosynthesis in rat tendon. Acta Physiol Scand. 1990;139:139–145.

30. [Van der Muelen JCH. Present state of knowledge and processes of healing in collagen structures. Int J Sports Med. 1982:3:4–8]

31. Potenza AD. Tendon and ligament healing. In: Owen R, Goodfellow J, Bullough P, eds. Scientific Foundation of Orthopaedics and Traumatology. London: Heinemann Medical; 1980: 300–305

oriented along the longitudinal axis of the tendon under influence of the normal load applied by its muscle. The strength of collagen fibers increases during this time with increasing cross-linking and fiber assembly. Furthermore the gradual shift to Type I collagen from Type III, also contributes to the strengthening of the tendon. These changes are well documented.

Ligaments

Large loads or a change of velocity over 5 mph can overpower the tensile resistance of ligament and result in injury. This usually manifests as a complete or partial tear or a stretch injury usually associated with multiple micro-tears. [32]

Grade I is characterized as a mild injury with no associated joint laxity.

Grade II is characterized as moderate injury with mild but clinically insignificant laxity.

Grade III is characterized as severe injury with significant laxity resulting from a complete tear of the ligament.

Ligament healing is achieved via the same basic mechanisms involving inflammation, repair, remodeling as discussed with tendons. Several factors impact the healing of a ligament including the severity of injury and the specific ligament involved. Ligaments do not have a good blood supply which complicates the ability for tissues to heal completely.

Ultimately, the healing outcome depends on several factors including ligament type and the associated local conditions. For example, the anterior cruciate ligament heals

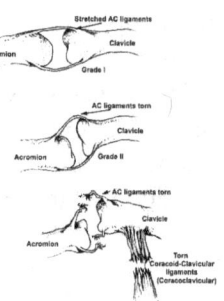

Figure 9

Grade I – III ligament tear of the acromio-clavicular joint.

(NOT the same as the Croft guidelines.)

---

32. Frank C, Amiel D, Woo S L-Y, et al. Normal ligament properties and ligament healing. Clin Orthop. 1885: 196:15–25

poorly.[33] [34] Another factor that influences the healing process is the stress acting on the scar. In tests using rabbits medial collateral ligament model, healing under tension has been shown to yield a scar that is characterized by its higher total collagen content and higher percentage of longitudinally-oriented collagen fibers compared to its non-tensioned counterparts.[35] It is particularly interesting to observe the effects of training and mobilization-immobilization regimens on the healing of ligaments. It has been shown that in the anterior and posterior cruciate ligaments of the cat knee there is a significant increase in the number of small-diameter fibrils and a notable decrease in the number of larger-diameter fibrils after prolonged exercise. In that study, however, the total cross-section area of fibrils of the exercised ligaments was smaller than that of controls, suggesting that exercise did not increase the tensile strength of the ligaments.[36]

On the other hand, the increase in number of smaller-diameter fibrils may be the factor decreasing stiffness of these ligaments.[37]

In support of this, immobilization of the rat medial collateral ligament has been shown to diminish the number of small-diameter fibers[38] and presumably leads to joint stiffness. The exact mechanism by which immobilization leads to joint stiffness has yet to be clarified. It appears that a combination of mechanisms may be involved. These include formation of intra-articular adhesions and an active contraction of ligaments by fibroblasts in a process mediated by contractile proteins. Human tissue responds in a like manner. Movement, stretching and

---

33. O'Donoghue DK, Frank GR, Jeter GL, et al. Repair and reconstruction of the anterior cruciate ligament in dogs: factors influencing long-term results. J Bone Joint Surg Am. 1971; 53:710–718

34. Noyes FR, McGinniss GH. Controversy about treatment of the knee with anterior cruciate laxity. Clin Orthop. 1985;198:61–76

35. Gomez MA, Woo SL, Amiel D, et al. The effects of increased tension on medial collateral ligaments. Am J Spords Med. 1991;1;19:347–354

36. Larsen N, Parker AW. Physical activity and its influence on the strength and elastic stiffness of knee ligaments. In: Howel ML, Perker AW, eds. Sports Medicine: Medical and Scientific Aspects of Elitism in Sports. Brisbane: Australian sports Medicine Federation; 1982;8:63–73

37. Tipton CM, Schild RJ, Tomanek RJ. Influence of physical activity on the strength of knee ligaments in rats. Am J Physiol. 1967;212:782–787]

38. Brinkley JM, Peat M. The effects of immobilization on the ultrastructure and mechanical properties of the medial collateral ligament of rats. Clin Orthop. 1986;203:301–308

joint mobilization during the healing stages results in more productive scar tissue formation with less chance of negative long-term pain and impairment.

Anatomy and Physiology in Summary

Soft tissue injuries will "heal on their own" over time. Whether or not the tissues heal properly, meaning as close as possible to pre-injury status, depends on intervention by the physical medicines. The developing adhesion fibers can potentially cause chronic problems or pain. This can typically be averted by the early intervention of the right type of rehabilitation treatment. Tissues heal more appropriately when stressed under gentle longitudinal traction to assist in proper alignment of collagen fibers.

Treatment of inflammatory symptoms with merely pharmaceuticals is not rehabilitation of tissue injury. Turning a blind eye to the process of inflammation and scar tissue formation is detrimental to the patient.

> **"Drugs never cure disease. They merely hush the voice of Nature's protest, and pull down the danger signals she erects along the pathway of transgression. Any poison taken into the system has to be reckoned with later on even though it palliates present symptoms. Pain may disappear, but the patient is left in a worse condition, though unconscious of it at the time."**
>
> ~Daniel H. Kress, M.D.

Motor Vehicle Collision Occupant Injuries

Infants

Newborns have their perfect little muscles just where they belong. Unfortunately these muscles lack *tonus*. Adults are able to sit or stand erect due to the subconscious effort of muscle tone. This is the normal state of balanced tension in the body tissues, especially the muscles. Partial contraction or alternate contraction and relaxation of neighboring fibers of a group of muscles hold the organ or the part of the body in a neutral functional position without fatigue. Tonus is essential for many normal body functions, such as holding the spine erect, the eyes open, and the jaw closed. Since newborns lack this tonus they are typically not able to lift their head or roll over for several months.

Additionally, unrestrained children have a greater potential for head injuries and ejection because of their different anthropomography. Meaning the head to torso ratio is significantly different than that of adults. Even without ejections the size of a child's heads in relation to their body creates unique and separate issues compared to adults; based on basic the physics of objects in motion. In a restrained child, the head is not restrained. Heads continue in motion even if the torso is restrained. Due to the lack of muscle tonus and development injuries can occur to the upper spine and head of children in MVCs.

For these reasons above newborns are especially susceptible to certain types of injuries. Acceleration-deceleration injuries for this age group come primarily in two forms, Non-Accidental Head Injury (NAHI) or Shaken Baby Syndrome in Motor Vehicle Collisions (MVC). The research on these two mechanisms of injury is intertwined.

The Shaken Baby Syndrome (SBS) is a common form of NAHI in which the victim is held by the torso or the extremities and violently shaken, causing abrupt uncontrolled head movements with a marked rotation component. [Whiplash or CAD-Cervical Acceleration Deceleration][39]

The most common cause of serious pediatric (age 0–16 yrs) spinal trauma is motor traffic incidents.[40] The 0–4 year age group has the highest proportion of serious injuries, at 47% of the group.[41]

There is some literature debate on which of these two mechanisms, SBS or MVC's, is actually the most common per age group. This book focuses on MVCs but we will use literature from both genres since the forces and injuries are nearly identical.

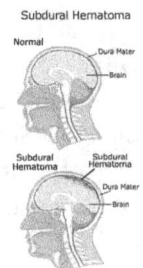

Figure 10

Infants are more susceptible than adults to intracranial injury from CAD injury. Because of the larger head to body ratio and the lack of tonus in their muscles, combined with the anatomic and developmental differences in the brain and skull of the young child, the mechanisms and types of injuries that affect the head differ from those that affect the older child or adult.[42]

Retinal detachment and subdural hematoma are common injuries from whiplash or CAD injuries involving infants. Rotational movement of the brain damages the nervous system by creating shearing forces. Shearing force causes diffuse axonal injury with disruption of axons and tearing of bridging veins. Vein injury causes subdural and subarachnoid hemorrhages, and is very commonly associated with

---

39. Review Article Shaken Baby Syndrome A Common Variant of Non-Accidental Head Injury in Infants Jakob Matschke, Dr. med.,*1 Bernd Herrmann, Dr. med.,2 Jan Sperhake, Dr. med.,3 Friederike Körber, Dr. med.,4 Thomas Bajanowski, Prof. Dr. med.,5 and Markus Glatzel, Prof. Dr. med.6

40. Pediatric Spinal Injury Type and Severity Are Age and Mechanism Dependent Spine; October 1, 2007, Vol. 32, No. 21, pp 2339–2347 Bilston, Lynne E. PhD; Brown, Julie BSc

41. Pediatric Spinal Injury Type and Severity Are Age and Mechanism Dependent Spine; October 1, 2007, Vol. 32, No. 21, pp 2339–2347 Bilston, Lynne E. PhD; Brown, Julie BSc

42. Position paper on fatal abusive head injuries in infants and young children. Case ME, Graham MA, Handy TC, Jentzen JM, Monteleone JA; National Association of Medical Examiners Ad Hoc Committee on Shaken Baby Syndrome. Department of Pathology, St Louis University Health Sciences Center, Missouri 63104-8298, USA. Comment in: • Am J Forensic Med Pathol. 2002 Mar;23(1):105; author reply 105–6.

retinal schisis and hemorrhages.[43]

These two mechanisms, SBS and CAD, cause the child's head to undergo acceleration-deceleration movements which may create inertial movement of the brain within the cranial compartment. Differential movement between the brain and skull may result in subdural and subarachnoid hemorrhages and traumatic diffuse axonal injury.[44] Similarly, a contrecoup injury could be observed under this type of injury. However, symptoms are more readily recognized in an adult patient. An infant study group post MVC found the perifalcine region was the most frequent site of intracrnial bleeding.[45] *(Figure 10)*

Since frontal collisions are the most common type of collision and statistically most injurious, rear facing seats are the most logical for infants. It is suggested that children remain rear facing as long as physically possible.

Infant car seats and child restraints are designed to distribute impact forces over a child's body in a more desirable manner than a seatbelt in a crash.[46] Rear facing infant car seats are helpful in that they prevent hyperextension of the cervical spine and distribute impact forces to the back and side of the head on a frontal impact or side impact. Picture this infant *(Figure 11)* with his car seat securely strapped in the back seat of a vehicle. In a frontal collision with a rear facing infant occupant is the most ideal position to reduce injury potential.

However, should the said vehicle suffer a rear impact collision by a second vehicle greater injury would happen.

---

43. Position paper on fatal abusive head injuries in infants and young children. Case ME, Graham MA, Handy TC, Jentzen JM, Monteleone JA; National Association of Medical Examiners Ad Hoc Committee on Shaken Baby Syndrome. Department of Pathology, St Louis University Health Sciences Center, Missouri 63104-8298, USA. Comment in: • Am J Forensic Med Pathol. 2002 Mar;23(1):105; author reply 105–6.

44. Leg Med (Tokyo). 2007 Mar;9(2):83–7. Epub 2007 Feb 2. Abusive head injuries in infants and young children. Case ME. St. Louis University Medical Center, Forensic Pathology, 3556 Caroline, St. Louis, MO 63104, USA. MCase@stlouisco.com

45. Pediatric Neurosurg. 2002 Nov;37(5):245–53. Infantile subdural hematomas due to traffic accidents. Vinchon M, Noizet O, Defoort-Dhellemmes S, Soto-Ares G, Dhellemmes P. Department of Pediatric Neurosurgery, CHRU de Lille, Lille, France. m-vinchon@chru-lille.fr

46. Wei Du, MPH; Andrew Hayen, PhD; Lynne Bilston, PhD; Julie Hatfield, PhD; Caroline Finch, PhD; Julie Brown, PhD Association Between Different Restraint Use and Rear-Seated Child Passenger Fatalities; Archives of Pediatric and Adolescent Medicine November 2008;162(11):1085–1089

Using a "low speed" collision, meaning a change of velocity (ΔV) less than 10 mph, we can compare data with an existing research sample from the San Diego Spine Research Institute (SDSRI). Imagine the *target vehicle* in which the infant is a passenger. The target vehicle is a large sedan and is stopped. It is struck from behind by the *bullet vehicle* a compact car traveling at 9.9 mph. Upon impact the energy from the bullet vehicle's mass in motion (P and KE) is transferred through the frame of the target vehicle directly into the occupants. Being a low speed collision and as per the video research of SDSRI there would likely be no visible damage to the vehicles (maybe a $50 bumper clip on the bullet vehicle) and no absorption of force. Thus all the forces were transferred through the frames of the vehicles directly into the occupants. Since the target vehicle was struck from behind and the infant car seat was rear-facing (as it should be), the body of this little infant would be rapidly jolted forward. In the study the Sedan goes from 0 to 6 mph instantly (ΔV).

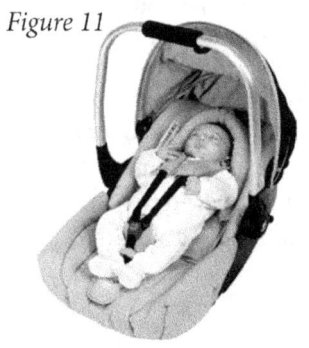

Figure 11

You can see by Figure 11 the infant's body is strapped in with a five-point harness to the car seat itself. The car seat is strapped to the vehicle. Since the Laws of physics state two masses cannot occupy the same space at the same time, the target vehicle has to vacate its original resting point and move forward to make room for the bullet vehicle. The body of the infant will move forward rapidly with the target vehicle. His head, *one-third of his body mass*, will be suspended for a split second as his body moves forward under the rapid change of Velocity (ΔV) and *g's* applied to it. This will cause an extreme flexion of the cervical spine. True, the car seat should prevent the head from hyper extending posterior as the head is whipped to catch up with the body. **The car seat does not, however, reduce any of the ΔV or *g's* experienced by occupants.** The occupant in the SDSRI study experienced a change of velocity of 6mph and a head acceleration of 13 *g's*. In this same research sample, the adult male was taken out of the study at this point due to injuries.

If an adult male sustained such injuries, more than likely, even in the protection of the car seat, the infant also sustained significant injury.

It is logical that an infant or child with their underdeveloped anatomy, large proportionate head and lack of muscle tone/strength would be more susceptible to injury. Unfortunately, an infant cannot communicate that it is having headaches or other symptoms but that does not negate the probability of injury.

> **View research footage at www.shetlin.com/media/**
>
> View "machine vs man_99-3" (This is copyrighted material and thus requires a password membership to view)
>
> The membership is FREE and I encourage you to view this research footage.

Diagnosing Infant Injury

A detailed history with the primary care giver is the first step in evaluating infants and children. Initially rule out serious injuries then look for the subtle forms of trauma. In that history specific details should be given regarding the child's demeanor, eating and sleeping habits. Obviously, excessive crying can indicate abnormalities, but other changes in the child's behavior can be an indication that something is wrong.

Physicians diagnosing infants must perform an adequate physical examination following the history. Palpation is a leading source of information during an examination. Gentle palpation can produce painful withdraws from an injured area. Older children can be examined with a do as I do exam meaning making the process more of a game. For example, turn your head this way touch your toes. Of course, observation—watching children play or interact while in the room with you—may be the most enlightening form of gathering information. Watch for limitations or protective actions.

The tragedy of infants and children involved in MVCs is that their soft tissue injuries are often over-looked or under diagnosed. "Delay in proper treatment or faulty treatment leads to adhesions about the facets and scarring about the capsular ligaments, persistent spasm, congestive lymph edema, fibrosis of muscles, swelling and eventually adhesions of nerves within the nerve root canals A neglected case enhances the degeneration of the intervetebral discs, and in addition, spurs formation in the lateral co-vertebral articulations, which on roentgenogram (X-ray) has come to be known as traumatic arthritis."[47] These degenerative changes may not

---

47. Seletz E. Whiplash Injuries - Neurophysiological Basis for Pain and Methods used for Rehabilitation; Journal of the American Medical Association, 1958

be noted on the injured child's X-rays until years or decades later.

Again, the most common cause of serious pediatric spinal trauma is motor traffic incidents.[48] Traffic-related incidents accounted for approximately one-third of all spinal trauma and half of serious injuries.[49] In research involving infants and children, spinal injuries were classified as serious if a fracture, spinal cord injury, *vertebral subluxation/* dislocation, or major *ligamentous injury* was present.[50]

"The upper cervical spine was more commonly seriously injured in young children, and the lower cervical spine was involved more often in older children."[51][52]

The welfare of the child must always have absolute priority.[53] Children should be checked immediately following any MVC. They should be examined for whiplash or CAD injuries regardless of the mechanism of injury by a physician specialized in diagnosis, treatment and rehabilitation of CAD injuries.[54] Parents may feel comfortable taking their children to a pediatrician, but a MVC occupant injury specialist visit is also recommended. In more severe cases, the ER doctor is the first to see the occupant/child after a MVC. In collisions thought to be less severe, the pediatrician will often be the first medical contact

---

48. *Pediatric Spinal Injury Type and Severity Are Age and Mechanism Dependent Spine;* October 1, 2007, Vol. 32, No. 21, pp 2339–2347 Bilston, Lynne E. PhD; Brown, Julie BSc

49. *Pediatric Spinal Injury Type and Severity Are Age and Mechanism Dependent Spine;* October 1, 2007, Vol. 32, No. 21, pp 2339–2347 Bilston, Lynne E. PhD; Brown, Julie BSc - Key points review by Dr. Dan Murphy

50. *Pediatric Spinal Injury Type and Severity Are Age and Mechanism Dependent Spine;* October 1, 2007, Vol. 32, No. 21, pp 2339–2347 Bilston, Lynne E. PhD; Brown, Julie BSc

51. *Pediatric Spinal Injury Type and Severity Are Age and Mechanism Dependent Spine;* October 1, 2007, Vol. 32, No. 21, pp 2339–2347 Bilston, Lynne E. PhD; Brown, Julie BSc

52. Stemper BD, yoganandan N, Pintar FA, Rao RD. *Anterior longituninal ligament injuries in whiplash may lead to cervical instability.* Medical Engineering & Physics 2006; 28: 515–524

53. Review Article *Shaken Baby Syndrome A Common Variant of Non-Accidental Head Injury in Infants* Jakob Matschke, Dr. med.,*1 Bernd Herrmann, Dr. med.,2 Jan Sperhake, Dr. med.,3 Friederike Körber, Dr. med.,4 Thomas Bajanowski, Prof. Dr. med.,5 and Markus Glatzel, Prof. Dr. med.6

54. Seletz E. Whiplash Injuries - Neurophysiological Basis for Pain and Methods used for Rehabilitation; Journal of the American Medical Association, 1958

following the trauma. It is recommended that these doctors refer to a certified specialist in MVC occupant injury for a second opinion and possible rehabilitative care. Emergency departments may rule out life threatening and other serious traumatic injuries. Due to administrative pressure or simply a lack of understanding regarding the mechanism of these injuries; few ER doctors or pediatricians refer to a specialist in this arena. Motor vehicle occupant injury certified professionals can diagnose and treat subtle traumatic injuries. This simple step in co-care of the patient could substantially decrease the statistical data that tells us over 50% of patients involved in auto crashes will likely develop chronic problems by the 2 year mark after the incident.

Of course, once a car seat has been involved in a MVC it must be replaced. If this is the case, and we fear the force of the crash was enough to possibly damage the car seat so it is no longer strong enough to function properly in a future impact, then it also needs to be standard protocol to have the precious cargo (the infant) checked by a physician who specializes in finding hidden soft tissue injuries.

Know that it is safe and appropriate to refer children to the chiropractic physician. The chiropractic profession, has sub-specialties include pediatrics. Chiropractic has been proven safe for over 115 years with numerous studies to document it. There are thousands of studies published and unpublished, ranging from asthma[55] to torticolis,[56] demonstrating how chiropractic is safe and effective for children. Chiropractic physicians treating children for soft tissue or other neuro-musculo-skeletal conditions is common place. Typically, with young children, an adjustment would consist of gentle pressure in the proper direction to mobilizing a fixated joint. The adjusting techniques used on newborns and infants are specialized vs. the "cracking" and "popping" style techniques frequently used on adults. There are over 130 chiropractic techniques. A skilled chiropractic physician will offer the most appropriate technique for each patient on an individual basis.

---

55. Asthma and Chiropractic Spinal Adjustments (Specific Manipulation) A literature review and research proposal, Jay Shetlin, DC St. George, UT USA/Lisbon, Portugal - http://www.shetlin.com/articles/asthma_review.pdf

56. Heart rate changes in response to mild mechanical irritation of the high cervical spinal cord region in infants Forensic Science International Volume 128, Issue 3, August 28, 2002, pages 168–176 L. E. Koch, H. Koch, S. Raumann-Brunt, D. Stolle, J. M. Ramirez and K. S. Saternus

In conclusion we have the following suggestions regarding child occupant safety:

- Drive paying attention/avoiding distractions; you have the most important cargo.
- Properly secure infant seat offering minimal movement
- Babies ride facing backwards as long as reasonably possible.
- Never place children near frontal airbags
- Keep all other object in the trunk.

Key Points by Dr. Shetlin

According to pediatric trauma research…

- "The most common cause of serious pediatric spinal trauma is motor traffic incidents."
- "Traffic-related incidents accounted for approximately one third of all spinal trauma and half of serious injuries."
- Spinal injuries were classified as serious if a fracture, spinal cord injury, vertebral subluxation/dislocation, or major ligamentous injury was present. Of age groups 0–16, the 0 to 4 -year age group had the highest proportion of serious injuries, at 47% of the group.

According to the review of Shaken Baby Syndrome…

- SBS is a non-accident version of a whiplash injury or CAD.
- The Mortality and Morbidity rate is the same as MVCs for the age Group 0–4 years old.
- SBS has been defined as an acceleration/deceleration or "whiplash" injury since 1971. This is the same terminology use in MVCs.
- SBS and whiplash are worse with a rotation component.
- The large head-to-body ratio combined with the immature/weak neck muscles of an infant or child make the likelihood of injury greater.
- Rapid shear forces are hazardous to neck muscles, ligaments, dura matter, brain tissue, spinal and intracranial blood vasculature.
- Abrupt deceleration with impact increases chance of injury.
- Severe or visible injuries prompt parents to have children seen by a doctor sooner.
- Lower brain stem injuries may not be noticeable at first but can be fatal over time.
- Many soft tissue injuries go unnoticed for long periods of time leading to greater problems to deal with later.
- Each child's case is individual and should be checked immediately for the welfare of the child.

RESEARCH

Auto Accidents	VS	Shaken Baby Syndrome
Pediatric Spinal Injury Type and Severity Are Age and Mechanism Dependent Spine; October 1, 2007, Vol. 32, No. 21, pp 2339-2347 Bilston, Lynne E. PhD; Brown, Julie		Pediatric Neurosurg. 2002 Nov;37(5):245-53. Infantile subdural hematomas due to traffic accidents. Vinchon M, Noizet O, Defoort-Dhellemmes S, Soto-Ares G, Dhellemmes P. Department of Pediatric Neurosurgery, CHRU de Lille, Lille, France. m-vinchon@chru-lille.fr
A. "The most common cause of serious pediatric spinal trauma is motor traffic incidents."		The most common cause of subdural hematomas (SDH) in infants is shaken-baby syndrome (SBS). The pathogenesis and natural history of infantile SDH (ISDH) are poorly documented, because in SBS, the date of shaking is usually imprecise and the assault is often repeated. Victims of traffic accidents (TA) form a study group close to experimental conditions, because the trauma is unique, witnessed and dated.
		Review Article Shaken Baby Syndrome, A Common Variant of Non-Accidental Head Injury in Infants, Jakob Matschke, Dr. med.,*1 Bernd Herrmann, Dr. med.,2 Jan Sperhake, Dr. med.,3 Friederike Körber, Dr. med.,4 Thomas Bajanowski, Prof. Dr. med.,5 and Markus Glatzel, Prof. Dr. med.6
B. "Traffic-related incidents accounted for approximately one third of all spinal trauma and half of serious injuries." DM		1. SBS or non-accidental head injury, which has high morbidity and mortality.
C. Of the total number of spinal injury cases found in this study, 30% were classified as serious and 70% were classified as minor.		2. The mortality can be as high as 30%, and up to 70% of survivors suffer long-term impairment.
		3. The shaken baby syndrome (SBS) is a common form of NAHI in which the victim is held by the torso or the extremities and violently shaken, causing abrupt uncontrolled head movements with a marked rotatory component. [whiplash or CAD]
D. This study found that "in children under 9, serious cervical spine injuries tend to be in the upper cervical spine (at or above C3), with the lower cervical spine becoming more frequently involved with increasing age."		4. In 1971 the British neurosurgeon Norman Guthkelch described two infants with subdural hemorrhage but no signs of external injury; as the cause, he suspected an acceleration-deceleration mechanism ("whiplash injury")
E. The 0- to 4-year age group had the highest proportion of serious injuries, at 47% of the group. "Traffic-related incidents were the most frequent cause of spinal injuries, irrespective of injury severity."		5. A number of anatomical features make infants particularly vulnerable to acceleration-deceleration events with a marked rotatory component, which typically occur on shaking [and MVCs]. The head is large in relation to the rest of the body and is not yet adequately supported and controlled by the weak, immature neck musculature. [important]
		6. Neuropathological investigation has revealed signs of corresponding focal damage in the lower brainstem. Even if a long-lasting episode of apnea is not immediately fatal, the resulting hypoxia causes cerebral edema with increased intracranial pressure and thus reduced cerebral blood flow, leading to a vicious circle of increasing cerebral hypoxia. The end result in such cases—depending on the delay before initiation of emergency treatment—is either protracted brain death or prolonged survival with serious deficits. [Children with CAD injuries may not show signs for some time.] Moreover, the shear forces that act on the immature brain during shaking result in traumatic diffuse axonal injury (DAI), which also participates in the development of cerebral edema.
		7. Patients with SBS have a poorer prognosis than victims of serious accidents; this can be attributed in particular to the differences in mechanism of injury and the frequent delay in taking the child to a doctor. [Kids in MVC who do not show immediate symptoms are too often not checked by a specialist in a timely fashion. See F]
F. "Children who sustain minor injuries and are not brought to hospital, but see a general practitioner or other health-care professional are not included in the sample." Therefore, this "data under-represents minor injuries."		8. Severe accidental head injuries are extremely rare in this age group and usually the result of falls from great heights or high-speed vehicle accidents. [Hmm…See Pediatric Spinal Injury Type and Severity Are Age and MechanismDependent Spine; October 1, 2007, Vol. 32, No. 21, pp 2339-2347 Bilston, Lynne E. PhD; Brown, Julie BSc]

Teens and Adults

In the United States, the leading cause of death among teenagers is motor vehicle collisions. The United States has more people under the age of 20 "operating heavy machinery" than any other country in the world. The result is a greater number of accidents, injuries, and deaths.

This is not to say that teen drivers are irresponsible, they are just young, easily distracted, inexperienced and their nervous system is underdeveloped. Physically and mentally, they do not have the reflexes and quick decision response necessary for operating heavy machinery (a vehicle) at high speeds in traffic. This is not to stereotype since there are clearly some adults with these same challenges, yet the majority of teenagers pose an increased risk.

> **TESTIMONIAL:**
>
> *After a car accident I had constant low back pain. I had tried Physical Therapy but with minimal results.*
>
> *Dr. Shetlin did a "Hands-on" examination and began treatment with adjustments, ice, e-stim, exercises and traction that together were very effective.*
>
> *I have had considerable low back pain relief as I have continued treatments.*
>
> *Don't knock it till you try it! Continue your treatments then decide - I love the results I am getting!*
>
> *~Mark*

A common misconception about infants, children and teens is that if they are not complaining or bleeding right after a trauma or MVC, they are "fine." A parent might say, "Oh, they're kids… they will be alright." The truth of the matter is that regardless of our age, when we sustain a spinal injury (whether or not it causes immediate pain) the degenerative process leading to arthritis starts at that point. Research from the Cervical Spinal Research Society published in 1989 documents that spinal trauma accelerates the degenerative process up to 6 time that of normal.[57]

Either way, developing problems are on the horizon when a proper course of rehabilitation is not followed immediately after an injury of this type. Examples from the practice of Dr. Shetlin, clearly show the magnitude of the above statements. Here is a comparative illustration of three different young women after experiencing MVCs; no other trauma was noted in their histories:

---

57. American Medical Association 2006, Acceleration of Degenerative Disc Disease Following Whiplash Injuries

- **CASE 1**—Patient sustained a CAD or whiplash injury from a MVC and was sore for just a few days. The pain subsided so she thought she was fine and did not receive any treatment. One year later (at the age of 25) she was experiencing neck pain and headaches.

- **CASE 2**—This patient sustained a whiplash injury from a MVC. She was seen by the ER and was prescribed muscle relaxers and anti-inflammatory medication for two weeks. The patient reports she felt fine after the two weeks. By the five year mark after her incident (now 25 years old) she had been experiencing headaches, neck pain and radicular symptoms into her upper extremities.

- **CASE 3**—This third case sustained a whiplash injury at the age of 15. She was a passenger in the vehicle. After the initial soreness wore off, she too though she had escaped the incident unharmed. Her parents thought, "She's young, kids are resilient, she will be fine." It wasn't until years later that she began experiencing neck pain, stiffness, loss of range of motion and headaches. When she finally presented to the chiropractic office (at the age of 25) X-rays clearly showed cervical curve problems and early degenerative disc disease.[58]

See pictures on next page.

---

58. The Cervical Spine Research Society Lippincott, 1989

When, Where and Why to Refer Auto Accident Patients

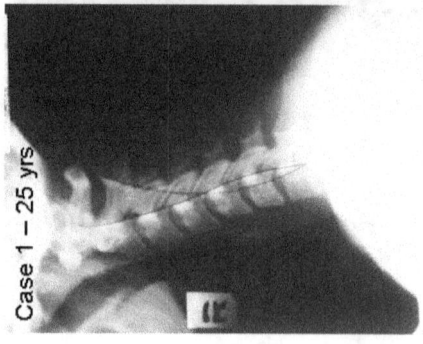

Case 1 – 25 yrs

1 year – post MVC
Symptoms: Headaches & neck pain
Visual findings: loss of cervical curve and anterior head carriage

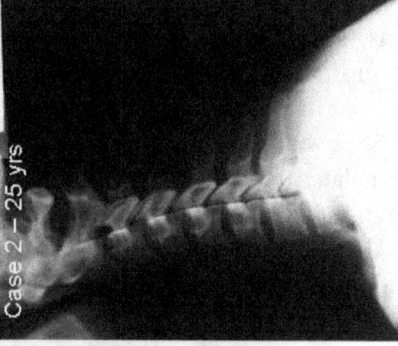

Case 2 – 25 yrs

5 year – post MVC
Symptoms: Headaches & neck pain, radicular pain in upper extremities
Visual findings: reverse of cervical curve and anterior head carriage

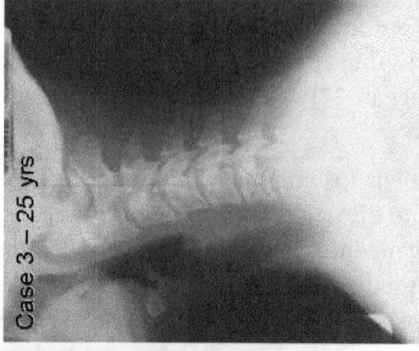

Case 3 – 25 yrs

10 year – post MVC
Symptoms: Headaches, neck pain, loss of range of motion
Visual findings: reverse of cervical curve, anterior head carriage and *degenerative disc disease*

It is important to note that there are several types of arthritis or joint/disc degenerative diseases. **Osteoarthritis such as seen here is not "part of growing old" it is due to trauma or joint dysfunction over time.**

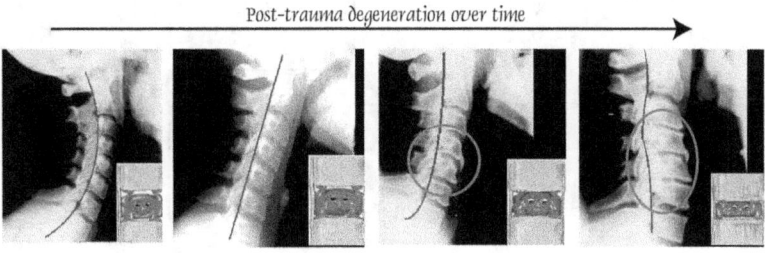

Post-trauma degeneration over time

Children and teens must receive proper medical/chiropractic work-up and medically necessary therapy following MVC or any traumatic injuries including but not limited to cervical acceleration/deceleration injury that can lead to early degenerative problems in the spine, thus negatively affecting their nervous system and overall health. This can lead not only to chronic pain, but affect communication between the brain and target organs/glands altering the individual's health and longevity.[59]

"Follow-up roentgenograms taken an average of 7 years after injury in one series of patients without prior roentgenographic evidence of disc disease indicated that 39% had developed degenerative disc disease at one or more disc levels since injury. The expected incidence of the general population is only 6%" In other words, when an individual experiences a trauma resulting in soft tissue damage they are "6.5 times more likely to develop degenerative disc disease."[60]

To put this into the simplest of terms; research shows we are "only as old as our spine and nervous system." In other word, since the nervous system controls everything in the body and is housed within the spine, premature degeneration of the spine can have a domino effect causing premature degeneration or pinching of the nervous system. Research dating back to the Windsor study in 1921 points out that degeneration of a nerve from the spine can and most likely will lead to organ disease or dysfunction. Thus, if we have organ disease and dysfunction due to nerve degeneration, caused by spinal degeneration we are actually aging prematurely. At 6.5 times the normal expected rate we would be "aging in dog years."

---

59. The Cervical Spine Research Society Lippincott, 1989

60. The Cervical Spine Research Society; *The Cervical Spine* -Lippincott, Williams & Wilkins 1989–2004

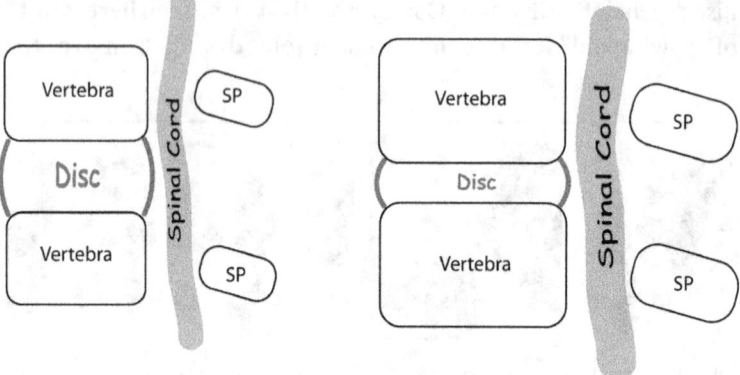

Size of Infant Disc compared to Vertebrae   Size of Adult Disc compared to Vertebrae

When compared with adults, infants, and children, teens anatomically have a number of characteristics that can contribute to the immediate perception of less or no injuries.

- Youthful spines have greater intervertebral disc spacing. This does allow for added overall flexibility.
- This may give rise to a larger intervertebral foramen as compared to the nerve root yielding a need for **excessive** inflammation before symptoms would present as compared to an adult who would not have that luxury, thereby, an adult would yield symptoms more readily.
- Depending on the age, bones may not be fully hardened from their original cartilaginous state.
- Again, depending on age, not all sites where bones fuse naturally may have taken place. This may allow for a small increase for flexibility as compared to an adult.

None of the aforementioned give reason for greater tensile strength of attaching soft tissues nor do they reduce the actual forces applied to the human body during a MVC. The fact remains that the soft tissues can only withstand so much force. The exact amount of force is unknown for a specific individual due to variables within individual anatomy. Notably, even low energy collisions are known to cause some amount of micro tears or trauma. Specific attention should be paid to the differences of anatomy between infants, children, teens and adults. These complicating factors are compounded by the nature of traumatic injuries and the fact that symptoms and pain may not be present for some time.

Adults

Since adults have less space between neighboring soft tissues, inflammation can more easily affect the nervous system yielding not only pain but radicular and somato-viseral symptoms.

Whiplash and Soft Tissue Injuries can be Nebulous

It is imperative that individuals involved in MVCs seek out or are referred to physicians trained to diagnose and rehabilitate the complicated and often near-invisible injuries related to car accidents.

The intake paperwork in an office where the treating doctors are certified in the diagnosis and treatment of these cases is vastly more detailed. This serves to gather the maximum amount of information regarding what took place, the forces and vectors involved in the collision, people who may have been injured, when and where symptoms originally started vs. symptoms expressed in late onset.

Detailed pain measuring systems included but not limited to visual analogue scales are typically used for each symptom to mark the starting point of their subjective symptoms. This information leads to determining traumatic injuries further leading the physician to an accurate diagnosis. This information will then be listed in a report that allows other healthcare providers, insurance claims handlers, and attorneys to understand the case.

Physical examinations must be detailed and include the appropriate neurologic, chiropractic and orthopedic tests in order to gather neurologic and musculo-skeletal involvement.

Some physicians use Surface EMG and other technology related instruments to help objectify neurologic involvement.[61]

---

61. Three separate studies, by researchers from 4 colleges and universities confirm reliability of the Insight SEMG.

The largest and most recent collaborative study by researchers from the Florida Atlantic University College of Biomedical Science and Life University found that the Insight(tm) surface EMG technology demonstrated excellent reliability. "This study revealed excellent inter-examiner and intra-examiner reliability of static paraspinal surface electromyography in a large number of subjects."

The SEMG reliability aspect of the study was presented at research conferences on two occasions, and published twice as part of proceedings of those conferences:

X-ray images are still the most cost-effective way to view osseous structures. With a minimum of two perpendicular images, much can be discovered. Often a trauma case requires oblique images and cervical flexion/extension images. Shortcuts miss important diagnostic information. For example, without flexion/extension films it is impossible to perform the AMA and Penning trauma line measurement protocols to properly diagnose ligament damage or instability. X-ray images can show osseous alignment which is helpful in combination with a detailed exam and history. X-ray images are not the image of choice for viewing soft tissues.

MRI is an effective way to help diagnose disc lesions since they so clearly illustrate the soft tissues. MRI does not clearly show ligament instability and most often the images are generated with the patient lying supine. Weight bearing images are much more telling in regards to spinal function and injury.

Motion X-ray is quite telling in regards to soft tissue injuries following an MVC. Similar to their less expensive counterpart, still X-ray images, motion X-ray best shows the osseous tissue. However, when motion

---

McCoy, M., Blanks, R., Campbell, I., Stone, P., Fedorchuk, C., George, I., Jastremski, N., Butaric,L. Inter-examiner and Intra-examiner Reliability of Static Paraspinal Surface Electromyography. Presentation. 2006 International Research and Philosophy Conference. Sherman College of Straight Chiropractic. Spartanburg, SC. November 3–5, 2006.

McCoy, M., Blanks, R., Campbell, I., Stone, P., Fedorchuk, C., George, I., Jastremski, N., Butaric,L. Inter-examiner and Intra-examiner Reliability of Static Paraspinal Surface Electromyography. Proceedings of the 2006 International Research and Philosophy Conference. Sherman College of Straight Chiropractic. Spartanburg, SC. November 3–5, 2006. J. Vertebral Subluxation Res. November 27, 2006

McCoy, M., Blanks, R., Campbell, I., Stone, P., Fedorchuk, C., George, I., Jastremski, N., Butaric,L. Inter-examiner and Intra-examiner Reliability of Static Paraspinal Surface Electromyography. Poster Presentation. Association of Chiropractic Colleges Research Agenda Conference. March 15–18, 2007.

McCoy, M., Blanks, R., Campbell, I., Stone, P., Fedorchuk, C., George, I., Jastremski, N., Butaric,L. Inter-examiner and Intra-examiner Reliability of Static Paraspinal Surface Electromyography. Proceedings of the Association of Chiropractic Colleges Research Agenda Conference. March 15–18, 2007. Journal of Chiropractic Education. Spring 2007.

is introduced we can clearly see the function of the supporting soft tissues such as ligaments and how well they are stabilizing the joint articulations in the spine and extremities.

Follow-up exams and X-rays are a vital part of true rehabilitation. They allow for objective documentation of progress and functional restoration. Without periodic follow-up exams and X-rays, we as physicians are simply treating symptoms and not truly tracking the recovery of the patient.

The second study was the basis of a dissertation by Hazel Faulkner, D.C., for an M.Sc. degree from the Institute or Medicine, Health and Social Care, University of Portsmouth.

"These results show that those subjects who have received recent and regular chiropractic adjustment have excellent reliability."

Faulkner HC: Test-retest reliability of sEMG paraspinal scans: A comparative study. Institute of Medicine, Health and Social Care. University of Portsmouth. M.Sc. dissertation. August 2006.

The third study was conducted at the New Zealand College of Chiropractic. It examined both reliability and pre/post sEMG changes.

"Under the conditions of this study, using the Insight...subluxation Station, it is concluded that sEMG is an objective measure of change which can be used as an assessment of patient progress."

Kelly S, Boone WR: The clinical application of surface electromyography as an objective measure of change in the chiropractic assessment of patient progress: a pilot study. Journal of Vertebral Subluxation Research 1998;2(4):1–7.

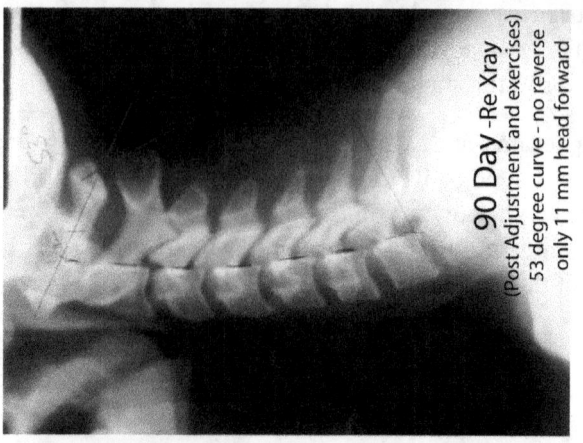

90 Day -Re Xray
(Post Adjustment and exercises)
53 degree curve - no reverse
only 11 mm head forward

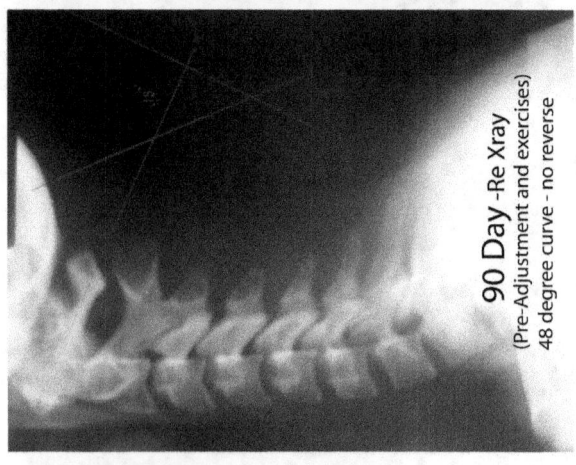

90 Day -Re Xray
(Pre-Adjustment and exercises)
48 degree curve - no reverse

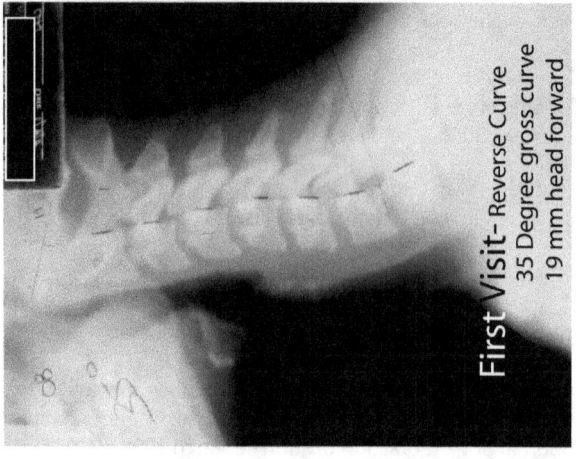

First Visit - Reverse Curve
35 Degree gross curve
19 mm head forward

Healthcare services are covered benefits by most automobile insurance policies. Many states require PIP (personal injury protection) or Medpay; some have it as an optional add-on. These are considered "no-fault" coverage and provide for the medical expenses of those involved in a MVC, regardless of who is at fault. The following 12 states have adopted "no fault" automobile insurance laws: Florida, Kentucky, Kansas, Hawaii, Michigan, Massachusetts, New Jersey, Minnesota, New York, Pennsylvania, Utah and North Dakota. See the following chapter for more information on automobile insurance.

When, Where and Why to Refer Auto Accident Patients

Insurance

In this day and age, insurance (all types combined) is typically the largest expense we as individuals have next to putting a roof over our head. The purpose of insurance is to create peace of mind and security from an unexpected loss of some kind. Auto insurance is no different.

The legal agreement between the insurance carrier and the insured is simple. The insured pays a premium each month in exchange for the agreed upon assistance if an unexpected loss should occur.

Once a motor vehicle loss or incident has taken place, the insured or "policyholder" is often in a state of disarray. Not only are there injuries to deal with, but there are also transportation issues, possible lost time at work, need for household services, and auto repair or replacement. Frustrated, most turn to their automobile insurance company for direction and help. Transportation is vital. If the insured is unable to drive to work, this affects their livelihood. They could lose their job. This can put an individual or family in a financial bind as their ability to pay their regular expenses and provide for their family becomes threatened. The incident can quickly turn from a question of injury recovery to how does he/she pay their bills and not lose their home?"

At a time of loss, policy holders are at their most vulnerable. Policyholders need to get paid as quickly as possible so they can get on with their lives. It is for this reason we buy insurance: come to the rescue when we're facing the kind of financial problems an unexpected loss can create.

Any italics in this chapter are direct quotes from David J. Berardinelli's book, "From Good Hands To Boxing Gloves."

Whiplash and Hidden Soft Tissue Injuries

The disadvantage policyholders face is that the insurance companies not only write the contracts but they act as the sole judge and jury of who gets paid, when and how much. This creates an enormous advantage for the insurance company over its policyholder. *There is a strong temptation for the insurer to take advantage of the policy holder.* In fact, many insured feel they are being taken advantage of.

Traditional insurance laws recognize this problem. Because the insurer controls the money the policyholder needs to recover from the loss, the insurer can delay payment to force the policyholder into accepting a smaller settlement than he or she is entitled to. Traditional insurance laws were adopted to "even the playing field." These rules have evolved over the last 100 years. They are intended to prevent insurers from taking advantage of their superior bargaining position over the policyholder.

However, few claimants know who or how to address issues they feel are not right regarding their claims. Most States have Insurance departments frequently staffed by former insurance employees. Their alliance is with insurance companies they were trained by and served for years. State Insurance Departments often have Insurance Fraud divisions that have been paid for by the citizens of that state. These fraud departments are designed to protect insurance companies. When there is a problem most claimants call their insurance adjuster and may be told something inaccurate. Trusting an insurance company insured usually do not appropriately document via a paper trail exactly what is going on with a claim. When an insured files a complaint with insurance department because there is not paperwork to the contrary the carrier response to the complaint is that this is simply a misunderstanding. It is critical to make detailed notes of who, what when, why and perhaps where any discussion. This is not the purpose of this writing to address the multitude of complications of this area alone.

There are two basic principles that need to be understood regarding how insurance works.

The **indemnity principle** which is unique to casualty insurance, offering the policyholder a payment of whatever is needed in order to restore an individual to the same financial position they were in after their loss as they were in prior to the loss, up to the policy's limit. This is different from a set benefit such as in a life insurance policy which pays a set fee upon a loss (death) of a policyholder.

*The **fiduciary principle** was also developed to balance the relationship between insurer and policyholder. This principle is based on the idea that insurers act like banks.*

Like banks, insurers accept their policyholders' money and keep it for them, promising to pay the full amount of their policy holders' covered losses. Promising to keep somebody else's money until they need it demands a high standard of conduct on the part of the person holding the money.

Banks can't tell you it's too much trouble for them to honor your withdraw slip, or ask you to withdraw less than you need. In the same way, insurance companies shouldn't intentionally delay your claim or ask you to accept less than your claim is worth.

These principles should give comfort to the informed policyholder. Sadly, most people, including policyholders and the front-line insurance agents who represent and sell policies, do not understand how a number of insurers will use shady techniques to beguile their policyholders after a loss in order to minimize recover thereby increasing shareholder profits.

Some of the techniques used include:

- Penalizing agents[62] who suggest policyholders seek a physician after an injury loss.
- Assessing damage to vehicles in low speed collisions (10 mph or less) and document in the file stating, "Because there is little damage to the vehicle, no one could have been injured." This makes it tempting for the insurer's medical adjuster or personal injury protection adjuster to refuse payment of medical bills. Surprisingly, neither adjuster has any medical training. Even more disturbing, it is **illegal** to refuse medically necessary treatment/payment until a policy limit is exhausted, (indemnity principle). However, using business techniques and other means of manipulations, these benefits can and have been cut off.

---

62. Insurance **agent** is often confused with an insurance **adjuster**. The agent is the nice friendly salesperson who offers you the policy and arranges to takes your money. The insurance adjuster is the insurance employee often appearing nice will gather information initially to start your claim. Later hands off to another adjuster who uses gathered information to delay, deny or reduce appropriate payments through skillful means.

- Recording calls with policyholders to document **any words** that may give reason **not to pay** out on their policy. Later the insurer or opposing insurer will use the policyholder's words against them. For example: "You said, 'I'm okay,' when we spoke with you just after the accident. Why should we pay these medical bills when you said you were 'ok?'" Or "We are not going to pay for your time and suffering because you told us earlier, 'I just want to get my medical bills paid and get my car fixed.'"
- Insurers are known to hire other physicians ("independent" medical examiners) to exam the patient and find reasons not to pay for previous care or discontinue current care...
    - In fact, there is no such thing as a true "independent" medical examiner (IME) because these doctors are directly or indirectly employed by the insurance company, which makes them an "**insurance** medical examiner." (IME) IME doctors are paid well by the insurer to save the insurer money. If they didn't, they would not have a job. The position of IME may be profession specific. Since a medical doctor should not negate the recommendations of a chiropractic physician nor visa-versa, IME doctors may be hired for each specialty. There are some areas in the health care field that present themselves as experts on this area and may be used more frequently. For example, neurologists and physiatrists are used more commonly to review many other specialties.
    - All the while the carrier stands back and implies we did not do this and IME made this decision. How long will the insurance doctor work if most of their opinions side on the side of injury and continued care? This is a very lucrative business for these doctors and thus raises significantly insurance company profits.
    - Many of these IME physicians are hired and use unethical or illegal techniques to reduce or freeze policyholder medical treatments. Another technique used is a "paper review." This is when the insurance company forwards whatever portion of the treating physician's note to one of their IME doctors or nurses, once again "fishing" for reasons not to pay or delay payment. Most states do not allow paper reviews. However, if the treating physician or the policyholder does not know the rules, then the scare tactic is successful causing the

policyholder to cease care prematurely and the doctor to accept less than normal expected fees for services rendered.
- Insurers contracting with outside services to, once again, filter through a case documentation, medical records, etc searching for any reason to "dispute, delay, or deny" and reduce payment.

Not all insurance companies follow these tactics but a surprising number do. The bottom line result is that insurance carrier increase profits at the expense of the injured or policy holders. If a carrier minimizes a personal injury protection (PIP) payment by $1000 the patient has a balance. Sooner or later the bill has to be paid. Often after credit complications and interest charges accrue. The question to ask is, "Why would any insurance company take such devious actions against its' own policyholders?" For this we need to understand how insurance works.

The "front door" is the insurance agent. Typically, the agent is our friend. They have the face to face time with a client. There is a trust and responsibility relationship that is shared. It is doubtful the insurance agents are aware of the underhanded financial strategies followed by the company they represent.

It is behind the "closed doors" of large office suites and corporate cubicles where the policyholder is viewed as a statistical opportunity of expense vs. bonus.

Insurance companies in decades past may have been less financially driven and more morally obligated to their policyholders. A structure was set and budgets were balanced in the best interest of both parties.

Every premium dollar a policyholder pays is divided into three parts:

- *Lost costs (about 70¢)*
- *Overhead and expenses (about 25¢)*
- *Profit (about 5¢)*

The percentage of each premium dollar an insurer pays out in claims is what the industry calls 'lost cost.' Lost costs are supposed to represent the amount of money the insurer expects to pay out in claims under all policies issued during a given year.

Overhead and expenses are the costs of doing business. These costs would include office space, postage, payroll, etc.

Profit is the return shareholders receive after all costs are met.

This has worked in the industry since the inception of casualty insurance. It is a business model that provides for it own survival, takes care of its employees and ethically balances the agreement and protection of its clients, the policyholders.

The Winds of Change

In the 1980s and 1990s, McKinsey worked on a number of projects for major insurance companies seeking to increase their profits. These included State Farm, United Services Automobile Association (USAA), Liberty Mutual, and apparently Hartford and Nationwide as well. During the mid-1980s, USAA invited interested insurance companies and their claim executives to its office in San Antonio for open discussions about how McKinsey redesigned its claim system. USAA credited McKinsey with saving the company. It openly shared information about McKinsey's redesign with its competitors.

In the early 1990s another business in the insurance industry wanted to find ways to improve its business model, in hopes to increase its profitability.

Allstate was a forerunner to hire a business "coach" or consulting firm not just to 'tune up' their protocols but to seriously 'over-haul' their business model. McKinsey & Company was hired by Allstate to transform them into a profit generating machine. The results have been devastating to the ethics and trust of the industry.

In the early 1990s, McKinsey preached its "greed is good" message loud and often in insurance management circles. McKinsey also preached the virtues of its star client—and the Wall Street darling—Enron Corporation. McKinsey knew a lot about Enron and its business model. McKinsey created it. In fact, McKinsey was Enron's principal advisor and strategist for over ten years before its collapse.

Allstate paid millions for the counsel of McKinsey and Company. Their investment yielded a fantastic return.

To put this into perspective, it took Allstate 63 years to build its 1994 surplus to 6.5 billion. Yet after adopting McKinsey's business model, Allstate more than tripled its surplus in only 12 years. That's even more remarkable because Allstate is telling the financial communities that since 1996 it has paid out 74% of its net income to shareholders.

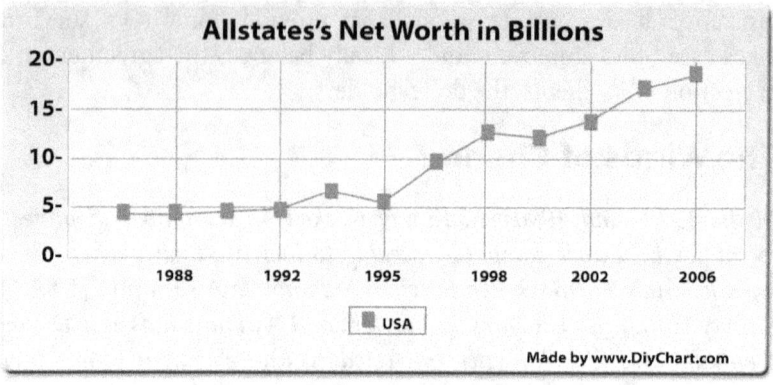

It is through tactics to lower the "lost cost" by leaving doctors, care givers and body shops underpaid for services and most importantly the clients left to receive a fraction of recovery funds they need, that Allstate was able to reduce claims paid and increase profits.

For example:

- Lost costs reduced by unethical tactics yield a payout (about 50¢ on the dollar)
- Overhead and expenses (about 30¢)
- Profit (about 20¢)

Once news of Allstate's profit success began to spread throughout the industry, more insurance companies decided the business model 'over-haul' was good for them as well. It spread through the industry like a cancer. A few companies heard the cries and complaints of their policyholders and moved away from this model back to the classic structure of service and commitment…most did not!

Today, patients need to know that if they do not get the care they need from doctors who know how to diagnose, treat, and document extremely well, it not only hurts them physically but financially. That is why there has been such a surge in the necessity of attorneys specializing in personal injury cases. An individual on their own is no match for the insurance giants and their perfected techniques to reduce policyholder payout. Even the personal injury attorney is at a considerable disadvantage if they do not have proper documentation from the doctors. If the individual injured is not at fault, the attorney needs to be introduced to the case early, before other McKinsey tactics are used such as recording calls and leading questions to document a patient/client verbally damaging their case.

Insurance Software

We will not fully address the software used by insurance companies in this book. In fact, this topic has volumes written about it and new professional experts to address it. To be brief, "Colossus" and similar programs are used across the country to calculate or generate a dollar value for a given injury. It is a simple case of 'garbage in, garbage out.' Based on the diagnoses and documentation turned in to the insurance carrier, some of the data is plugged into the program and 'Voila'…a near bulletproof defense is generated to support minimal settlement for their loss.

From an insurance business standpoint, software of this nature is a brilliant tool. From the doctor, the patient (the insured) and an attorney point of view, it neglects the individual as a whole and the abundance of variables present in each case. Leaving society, the patient and others to pick up the costs.

Personal Injury Protection and Med-Pay Insurance

How They Work

Unless an individual is an insurance adjuster or attorney, chances are they lack the understanding of exactly how PIP or MED-PAY insurance works. For this reason I have asked Mr. Jeff Metler, Esq to explain the basics of PIP: http://metlerlaw.com

Understanding Utah PIP

By Jeff Metler, Esq

Throughout the initial days after an auto accident, an individual will frequently hear the term PIP used in various conversations. PIP stands for Personal Injury Protection. The terms PIP Benefits, No-Fault Benefits, and MedPay Benefits are all synonymous. PIP payments for initial medical expenses, wage loss, and household services will be made under the auto insurance policy of the car you were riding in (or driving) regardless of who was at fault for the collision. (These services can include, but are not limited to, ambulance service, hospital or nursing services, physical therapy or chiropractic care, surgical, X-ray, dental, or other rehabilitative services.)

A claim for these benefits should not increase your insurance premiums. An individual's insurance carrier will seek reimbursement from the negligent driver's insurance at a later time. A skilled Personal Injury attorney can facilitate this procedure for you. If you were a passenger when you were injured, you should be covered under a car owner's policy as long as they have/had insurance that contains PIP benefits.

To begin receiving these PIP benefits, you must complete a PIP application sent by the insurance company. No payments will be made until the insurance claim is open and your PIP application is received by the insurance company. If you do not receive a PIP application within one week of notifying the insurance company, let your attorney know immediately.

If you have any other questions filling out the PIP application, contact your attorney. **Keep all facts about the collision and your injuries very basic (e.g. neck and back injuries).** You must sign the release to have them obtain your medical records or they will not pay any benefits. You do not need to sign the release to have them obtain your employment records if you are not making a claim for lost wages.

Your insurance adjuster may want to take a recorded statement. Please discuss that with your attorney before giving the statement. *You may discuss the processing or your PIP benefits directly with your insurance adjuster, however,* **do not discuss any facts of the collision or extent of your injuries with the adjuster.**

If your insurance policy has PIP benefits, you are entitled to at least $3,000.00 in the state of Utah for reasonable and necessary medical expenses.[63] The applicable policy may have a higher PIP amount. Your attorney or your insurance company will notify you of the amount to which you are entitled. To obtain medical benefits under PIP, copies of your itemized bills must be sent to the insurance adjuster.

CAUTION: *Insurance companies only pay for what they consider to be "reasonable and necessary" expenses. You and your doctor may believe a certain medical expense is necessary but the insurance company may disagree with you. This situation often arises from preexisting conditions or chiropractic treatments that go beyond the insurance company's "guidelines." Your attorney will assist you in attempting to collect for these expenses but caution should be taken when your chiropractic visits exceeds thirty (30) visits, or when large medical expenses are incurred such as MRIs, CT scans, or when your injuries are in the areas of the body that have had preexisting medical problems. If you have any questions regarding your treatment plan, or other medical questions, please call your attorney.*

---

63. Note: Most "no fault" states have a minimum requirement of $15,000 to $25,000. Utah has been at $3000 since 1967. The Utah State minimum PIP requirement seriously needs to be increased to keep up with the medical costs of our modern society.

If the adjuster feels your treatment is not reasonable and necessary, you may be required to be seen by a physician hired by the insurance company. These examinations are referred to as Independent Medical Examination or IME.

In Utah, The PIP provider will pay the lesser of $250 per week or 85% of any loss of gross income and loss of earning capacity from inability to work for a maximum of fifty-two (52) weeks after the loss, but most policies have an initial waiting period of three (3) days. Please consult the respective PIP policy for details. PIP benefits will also cover a special damages allowance, not exceeding $20 per day for a maximum of 365 days, for services actually rendered or expenses reasonably incurred for services that, but for the injury, you would have performed yourself for the household. This benefit need not be paid by the insurance company for the first three (3) days after injury, unless your inability to perform these services continues for more than two (2) consecutive weeks. Please refer to the respective PIP policy for details.

PIP Benefits will also pay for funeral benefits and what is referred to as a "survivor benefit" if an injured party dies as a result of the injuries sustained in the accident. PIP Benefits will pay funeral, burial or cremation benefits, not to exceed a total of $1,500.00* for a deceased person. PIP will also pay compensation on account of the death of a person, payable to his or her heirs, in the total amount of $3,000.00*.

All details explained are examples and do not apply to all cases. All benefits available are dependent upon the policy in effect at the time of the accident.

USAA Document Processing
Auto Injury Solutions
PO Box 5000
Daphne, AL 36526

RE: Patient ▓▓▓▓▓▓ - Appeal

To Whom it May Concern:

Please review the documentation originally submitted, the "Initial Report" and the "Croft guidelines." The report for both clearly state that both patients had seen a health care provider prior to visiting our office. Explanation for gap of care was also addressed. Providing a $350 initial report on each patient at NO CHARGE seem to reduce the likelihood of your specialist actually reading it. I will include my charge and re-submit the reports for your review.

> SPECIFIC ITEM OF DISPUTE:
>
> Peer review of paperwork to determine necessity of care.
>
> I am concerned by the fact that USAA continues to deny payment of diagnostic procedures performed by a primary care physician who actually sees the patient, yet USAA pays paper review physicians who have NOT seen the patient to come up with reasons NOT to take care of their contracted clients and the bills submitted by providers.

In regards to the conduct of USAA:

1. According to Utah Code 31A-22-309 Section 31A-22-307

- Payment of benefits shall be paid as incurred.

- Payment is overdue if not paid within 30 days after the insurer receives reasonable proof of the fact and the amount of expenses incurred during the period.

- If the insured fails to pay the expenses when due, these expenses shall bear interest at the rate of 1 1/2 % per month after the due date.

- The person entitled to the benefits may bring an action in contract to recover expenses plus the applicable interest. If the insurer is required by the action to pay any overdue benefits and interest, the insurer is also required to pay reasonable attorney's fee to the claimant.

Dr. R. Jay Shetlin   10456 S. Redwood Rd;. South Jordan, UT 84095   801 446-5100

In regards to the Physicians you choose to employ in order to justify denial of care:

The Utah Chiropractic Physicians Association considers "paper reviews" of patient files as unethical. It is bordering on illegal; thus employing physicians to perform paper reviews are an unacceptable means of denying claims in our state and put the license of those physicians in jeopardy.

According to the Utah Umbrella Act regarding Doctors of Chiropractic from the website of the Department of Professional Licensing, your physicians are performing paper reviews deemed "unethical" by their State Association which is "unprofessional conduct."

- Under the Umbrella Act 58-1-501-2B

 (2) "Unprofessional conduct" means conduct, by a licensee or applicant, that is defined as unprofessional conduct under this title or under any rule adopted under this title and includes:

 (a) violating, or aiding or abetting any other person to violate, any statute, rule, or order regulating an occupation or profession under this title;

 (b) violating, or aiding or abetting any person to violate, any generally accepted professional or ethical standard applicable to an occupation or profession regulated under this title;

I politely and professionally suggest USAA cease and desist delaying or denying medically necessary treatment for their insured, as well as, discontinue paying hired physicians to engage in activities that are deemed unethical and display unprofessional conduct by their peer association.

Sincerely,

R. Jay Shetlin
Chiropractic Physician and Author
Certified Motor Vehicle Occupant Injury Specialist

Dr. R. Jay Shetlin   10456 S. Redwood Rd;. South Jordan, UT 84095   801 446-5100

Treatment Guidelines

Maximum Medical Improvement

Maximum Medical Improvement (MMI) is defined as "a condition or state that is well stabilized and unlikely to change substantially in the next year, with or without medical treatment. Over time, there may be some change; however, further recovery or deterioration is not anticipated."[64] The current edition of the American Medical Associations (AMA) Guides to the Evaluation of Permanent Impairment defines MMI as, "the point at which a condition has stabilized and is unlikely to change (improve or worsen) substantially in the next year with or without treatment. While symptoms and signs of the condition may wax and wane over time, further overall recovery or deterioration is not anticipated."[65]

There are many different names like or similar to the MMI concepts that vary depending on organizations, states and or providences. [66] Professionals must learn and use terms that are common to their area or systems. If there is no known standards I suggest you use the AMA Guides as the standard.

---

64. American Medical Associations Guides to the Evaluation of Permanent Impairment 5th Edition. p 601

65. American Medical Associations Guides to the Evaluation of Permanent Impairment 6th Edition. p 612

66. Other terms include, but are not limited to—ascertainable loss, end of healing, fixed and stable, maximum cure, maximum degree of medical improvement, maximum medical healing, maximum medical recovery, maximum medical rehabilitation, maximum medical stability, medical end result, medical stability, medical stabilization, medically stable, medically stationary, permanent and stationary, and stable and ratable.

An example of another system is Utah's 2006 Impairment Guides as published by the Utah Labor Commission. "Medical stability, permanent and stationary, maximum medical improvement, (MMI), or fixed state of recovery, refers to a date in which the period of healing has ended and the condition of the worker is not expected to materially improve or deteriorate by more than 3% Whole Person in the ensuing year. It is important to note that medical stability may not be used to terminate necessary medical care. The date of medical stability and the date when the worker qualifies for an impairment rating can be two separate dates."[67] This concept is important because there are some in the insurance world who state that if a person has reached MMI or has received an impairment rating, no further treatment is medically necessary. While this may be true in some cases it is not correct in all cases. This is certainly a point in patient care where the physician must make medical decisions and the practice must make business decisions of the future of billing. This area leads to great difficulties in complicating PI cases. It is strongly suggested that additional training and procedures occur. Many bodily injury cases have taken a serious downturn because of ignorance to this topic.

It is important to note that if treatment is withdrawn, and the patient's clinical status becomes worse, the patient has not achieved maximum medical improvement. Such a scenario indicates that additional scheduled treatment is reasonable and necessary.

Treatment Protocols and Guidelines

There are specific medical treatment protocols and guidelines in place for most anything from swallowing a penny to a gunshot wound.

Injuries caused from MVCs are no different. The simple ones such as bumps, bruises and scrapes are like any other. Skin burns from an airbag or a broken bone have simple protocols. Serious injuries like internal bleeding puncture wounds or spinal cord injuries require a trauma unit. Trauma units are skilled physicians and nurses with a series of intense treatment guidelines and protocols related to each specific type of injury.

It is the soft tissue and hidden injuries from MVC where guidelines and protocols get fuzzy. For example, most emergency rooms see auto injury patients who are not injured seriously enough to admit to the

---

67. Utah's 2006 Impairment Guides as published by the Utah Labor Commission page 22

hospital with only a cursory exam, minimal X-rays and, infrequently, a scan. After internal bleeding and fractures are ruled out, the patient is sent home with a two week prescription of off work for 3-days, anti-inflammatory and muscle relaxant medication.

With all the forces the patient's body just experienced in the collision and the high probability of soft tissue injuries, the treatment protocol is simply to help placate or calm the current often-underdeveloped symptoms—not to diagnose and treat the injuries.

The patient is rarely if ever referred to a specialist. At best, if the ER patient asks for a referral it is simply suggested they see their primary care physician. Upon interviewing several ER doctors I have made a troubling discovery. **It is not that the doctors are unwilling to refer to specialists but that many hospital administrators prevent the ER doctors and staff from referring to anyone.** This is a problem that needs to be addressed since the statistics clearly show that years following a MVC, approximately 40-60% of auto injury victims are left with chronic pain. Furthermore, 10% of those develop some level of disability. A staggering number of these could be prevented if the patient simply received a proper referral early on, within the first 72 hours. Without soft tissue diagnosis and rehabilitative care, early scar tissue sets in and many symptoms become permanent. This can then leads to impairments followed by long term disability.

National Institute for Neurological Disorders Guidelines

The National Institute for Neurological Disorders and Stroke suggests the following approach to the treatment of whiplash associated disorders. As discussed, this is commonly used by ER doctors in cases not admitted to the hospital and also used by general practitioners. **Treatment for individuals with whiplash may include pain medications, nonsteroidal anti-inflammatory drugs, antidepressants, muscle relaxants, and a cervical collar** [68] **(usually worn for 2 to 3 weeks).** Range of motion exercises, physical therapy, and cervical traction may also be prescribed. Supplemental heat application may relieve muscle tension.[69]

---

68. While soft cervical collars are widely used, research has shown they have little value. Some research indicated soft collars can lead to long term problems.

69. http://www.ninds.nih.gov/disorders/whiplash/whiplash.htm

Chiropractic, Physical Medicine and Physical Therapy Guidelines

Since the 1980's there have been attempts to organize and implement treatment guidelines to help in this area. Physical therapy used to require a medical prescription. At present, medical doctors write prescriptions for physical therapy however they typically do not know what the physical therapist knows and so they dictate treatment frequency and duration based on limited understanding. Doctors of chiropractic might do likewise. Fortunately, more physical therapists are gaining the freedom to write their own prescription of care.

Chiropractic physicians who treated automobile injury patients in decades past would see a new auto occupant injury patient, take a history, perform an exam and take X-rays. Following that, they would write a prescription for chiropractic care with or without massage and physical therapy. However, each doctor would come up with their own random number of treatments needed for a particular patient. There were no guidelines or accurate protocols, and so any medical or any chiropractic doctors would likely come up with completely different treatment recommendations should they examine the same traumatized patient.

TESTIMONIAL:

I was the passenger in a car accident while on vacation in California. After returning home I was getting more and more sore. A lawyer friend said I should be checked by a doctor so I went to the emergency room…after a bill for over $1900 I received no treatment, no care plan and nothing but a two week prescription of muscle relaxors and pain killers. I was pissed!

After two days of laying around at home in pain I got on the internet and happened across a certified auto accident specialist chiropractor.

With treatment I started feeling so much better! The doc helped me with my work so my boss would understand why it was difficult for me to lift or stand too much. The treatment went way beyond just treating my pain. The office had physical therapy and massage and even taught me how to eat better and sleep better to heal faster!

I was the victim in this accident and the insurance company in California was trying to screw me over.

I am glad I found the right office with the right staff to help my case or I would have been stuck with the bills.

~Steve

The Mercy Guidelines

In 1993 the Guidelines for Chiropractic Quality Assurance and Practice Parameters, more commonly known as the Mercy Guidelines were developed by a thirty five member commission initially sponsored by the Congress of Chiropractic State Associations (COCSA) The Mercy conference was developed in a closed session by these thirty five panel members without input from the health care profession at large. No explanation was given as to how the thirty five individuals were selected. Historically, very few chiropractic organizations accepted the Mercy Guidelines. As more details came to light regarding them, these standards were dropped rather quickly. On the other hand, many automobile insurance companies readily accepted them and used them against the injured, including for bodily injury claims and trials.

The purpose of these guidelines was to offer doctors some foundational grounds and guidance for treatment frequency. Page 117 of the Mercy document states, "Their purpose is to assist the clinician in decision-making based on the expectations of outcome for the **uncomplicated case**. They are not designed as a prescriptive or cookbook procedure for determining the absolute frequency of care and the duration of treatment/care for any specific case."

Page IV offers a general disclaimer stating, "The ultimate judgment regarding the propriety of any specific procedure must be made by the practitioner in light of the individual circumstances presented by each patient."

These guidelines focused on "uncomplicated" cases which makes them less than ideal for applying to MVC cases because there are so many complicating factors. MVC occupant injuries (MVCOI) are by definition complicated. There is no place for MVCOIs in the Mercy Guidelines. Factors such as head position, vector, pre-existing conditions, and mass of the target and bullet vehicle make each MVC unique, and therefore can complicate both the diagnosis and treatment of injuries.

Regrettably, the Mercy guidelines lacked clarity for diagnosing severity of the injuries, categorizing the injuries and treatment of injuries. Regardless, they were rushed into the hands of insurance companies to set a standard of care for the medical/chiropractic treatment of patients. Being heavily misquoted or "taken out of context" the Mercy

Guidelines became a poor standard for years, forcing doctors to limit traumatic patient care. Frequently MVCOI patient care was limited to as little as 10 to 14 visits per case. This seriously inhibited proper rehabilitation of MVCOIs.

Confusion over the limitations and proper use lead to a rebuke of the Mercy Guidelines in 2000 by most state associations. Currently the Mercy Guidelines are rarely used by treating physicians and only seen in court cases as defense grounds *against* injured parties.

The Quebec Task Force Guidelines

"The health costs of whiplash-associated disorders (WADs), while not as high as the cost of low back pain, affects approximately 3 million Americans each year. North of the border, the province of Quebec in 1987 paid out over $18 million Canadian health care dollars for whiplash injuries. That significant expenditure moved the Quebec Automobile Insurance Society to fund a major study on whiplash-associated disorders.

It is important to note: Canada and the US have two entirely different insurance structures, different currency values and often times, different medical treatment protocols. Yet these guidelines were used in US court system countless times to lower payment by insurance companies to their insured and treating US physicians

The Society (state health care) approached Walter Spitzer, MD, MPH, FRCPC, professor of medicine at McGill University, to gather an international team of whiplash experts. Dr. Spitzer formed the Quebec Task Force on Whiplash Associated Disorders, an eighteen member group that included chiropractic researcher J. David Cassidy, DC, PhD, FCCSC. Their monogram was published in the April 15, 1995 supplement of the Spine journal (to order a copy, call 800-638-3030, The full report is available directly from the SAAQ)

The literature review was particularly rigorous, lasting nearly two years and encompassing 10,382 research papers on the treatment of whiplash. Of the 10,382 studies only 1,204 met the preliminary screening criteria, many because they were case histories without any validation of treatment efficacy. From there, the panel whittled down the studies to a select core group of 294. These studies were then rated for relevance and scientific merit. Only 62 of the 294 (21 percent) made the final cut and were deemed acceptable to the task force. This lack of acceptable research would ultimately leave many forms of whiplash treatment without any evidence of efficacy." [70]

Ideally QTF is intended to help insurers estimate a reasonable medical and rehabilitation expenses for a person who has sustained a whiplash injury.

Besides determining an accurate diagnosis, objective testing procedures assist in personal injury (PI) case management. Based on observed visual range of motion restrictions during the physical evaluation, and/or bilateral strength differences in the upper and/or lower extremities, and abnormal X-ray findings, objective computerized/measured testing should next be used to evaluate the spine and upper extremities. The area of testing can be based on patient symptoms and symptomatic patterns. Additionally, physician education, training and insight are important in determining further testing. Areas specifically to be tested include spinal range of motion, grip and/or pinch strength and/or computerized muscle testing. The graphed results can be used to quantify observed and functional restrictions. This data is used to help determine a more accurate diagnosis that then leads to appropriate treatment protocols and ultimately Maximum Medical Improvement.

There are both positive and negative aspects of the Quebec Task Force guidelines. One of the more negative aspects stems from the fact that the study was originated and paid for by the insurance industry in an effort to reduce the expense of pay-outs insured clients would receive for their whiplash associated disorder injuries related to MVCs. The guidelines have been used in court too often for that very purpose: to limit or reduce medical treatment to the injured or reduce payment for the medical treatment received by those injured in a MVC. They have even been quoted and used in US court cases. Another negative aspect relates to the fact that the guidelines are pain based. This relates back to the source of funding for these guidelines. Some whiplash care was addressed specifically for pain reduction rather than full rehabilitation.

QTF fell under intense scrutiny and is certainly controversial; however, it is too often referenced in court, even with its blatant flaws. This misuse is to claim maximal medical improvement before a patient in fully recovered.

---

70. http://www.chiroweb.com/archives/13/13/28.html

On the up side, the Quebec Task Force guidelines make an effort to qualify whiplash and soft tissue injuries with a grading system. Four grades of Whiplash-Associated Disorder were defined by the Quebec Task Force on Whiplash-associated disorders (WADs):

- **Grade 0:** No neck pain, stiffness, or any physical signs are noticed
- **Grade 1:** Neck pain, stiffness or tenderness, no physical signs noted by examining physician.
- **Grade 2:** Neck pain, stiffness or tenderness, examining physician finds decreased range of motion and point tenderness in the neck.
- **Grade 3:** Neck pain, stiffness or tenderness plus neurological signs such as decreased deep tendon reflexes, weakness and sensory deficits.
- **Grade 4:** Neck complaints and fracture or dislocation, or injury to the spinal cord.

According to the recommendations made by the Quebec Task Force, "treatment for individuals with whiplash associated disorders grade 1–3 should include manipulation, mobilizations and range of motion exercises." [71] This is a commendable natural approach to help the body in the healing process.

The task force also concludes that, "non-narcotic analgesics and non-steroidal anti-inflammatory drugs may also be prescribed in the case of WAD 2 and WAD 3, but their use should be limited to a maximum of 3 weeks. [72] This is vital. Medication is not a replacement for chiropractic manipulation, mobilization and range of motion exercises; it is used to help in reducing the acute "symptoms" while the manual therapies help prevent unwanted scar tissue from developing following the injury.

Overall the Quebec Task Force guidelines are a step in the right direction in the evolution of treatment protocols for WAD and soft tissue injuries; however, they are nowhere near the best available choice.

---

71. Gurumoorthy D, Twomey L (1996). "The Quebec Task Force on Whiplash-Associated Disorders". Spine 21 (7): 897–8.

72. Gurumoorthy D, Twomey L (1996). "The Quebec Task Force on Whiplash-Associated Disorders". Spine 21 (7): 897–8.

The Croft Guidelines

The Croft guidelines have been available for Doctors of Chiropractic Since 1993. This was the same year the Mercy guidelines were released and rapidly pushed into the spotlight. The Croft guidelines, however, are based on 25 years of research of injured occupants. The Croft guidelines also offer a much more detailed diagnostic categorization system that correlates to the suggested treatment guidelines for frequency and duration. A significant factor in the work of Dr. Croft and the Spine Research Institute of San Diego is they have no ties to the insurance industry, thus providing a non-bias opinion. These standards have become the leading guide for physicians in whiplash diagnosis and chiropractic treatments.

With their focus on the science of applied physics, occupant injuries, how the body heals, and long-term outcomes, the Croft guidelines have become the national standard of choice, supported by many states as well as published in other countries.

The Croft guidelines categorize the following:

- The **type** of collision that took place to help distinguish vector complexity.
- The **stage** of injury, which is determined by the amount of time passed since the onset of injury. This is an important component because the later the stage the more scar tissue is likely to have formed, which reduces the patient's potential for maximum improvement.
- The **grade** of injury, which can only be properly determined following a detailed history, Orthopedic-Neurologic-Chiropractic examination combined with the proper reading and measurements of the appropriate X-ray images.
- The **complicating factors** which must be calculated into the equation giving the physician, the patient, the insurance companies and any parties involved in a litigation case, a better understanding of why the recovery may be more difficult than expected.
- The **treatment recommendations**, which are based on a compilation of these four factors, especially the grade of injury.

This is why a physician should be properly trained and tested to certify in this field so the diagnosis and grading of the injury is true, accurate and reproducible between other specialists.

Type

Type I or primary rear end collision is one of the most common causes of motor vehicle injuries seen in and out of the emergency room. Rear impact comprises approximately 10% of crash types. The nature of this type of impact leaves the occupant unprepared to guard or properly brace for impact. Even if they are aware of the oncoming collision and tense up or push themselves rearward into their seat there are still several other complicating factors that can lead to serious injury even in a low speed impact.

Type II or primary side impact collision leaves little deceleration space between the bullet vehicle[73] and the target vehicle.[74] In addition, there is little space between the bullet vehicle and the occupants of the target vehicle. If the driver of the target vehicle is struck squarely in the driver's side door there may be less than six inches of crush space between the door of the target vehicle and the driver. Less deceleration space or crush space combined with a side impact can complicate the injury. Further complications arise if the driver is turned to look at the bullet vehicle.

TESTIMONIAL:

A few years ago I was involved in a car accident and went to a Certified Specialist who helped me make a great recovery.

This year I was the passenger in a new accident. We all went to the Emergency Room and all they told me was to take Tylenol for my headaches and ice my swollen head at home. It was just shy of an invitation to "hurry up and get out of there." I didn't even get a referral to someone who specializes in auto accident injuries. I was not impressed!

I remembered how helpful chiropractic was with my whiplash before. I called my chiropractor's office and made an appointment. The history and exam were thorough! They even took x-rays. It was nice going where people know what they are doing and have a sense of humor to deal with a jokester like me! The whole experience was great!

~Joleen

Type III or primary frontal impact collisions have a split of pro's and con's. Since the driver is usually paying attention ahead they are more

---

73. Bullet Vehicle is the vehicle that causes the crash. In a Type I crash the bullet vehicle is the one that rear ends the target vehicle.

74. Target Vehicle is the vehicle that is rear ended by the bullet vehicle in a Tyoe I vector.

likely to see a collision coming and can brace, offering a slight aid in decreasing the change of velocity and g's at the moment of impact. Unless the driver or passenger is smaller, or has the seat in an overtly forward position, there should be 16 inches or more of space between their face, chest and the steering wheel or dashboard. This distance prior to impact reduces occupant/airbag contact, reducing injury potentials from the airbag. However, this does not negate the possibility for injury. Seatbelts save lives but increase cervical acceleration/deceleration injury or whiplash. The sudden stop of the body while the head remains in forward motion often results in whiplash and is likely to cause soft tissue injuries.[75][76] In an impact over 10 mph ΔV or greater, the airbag in modern cars are likely to deploy. Depending on the position of the occupant, the airbag may help prevent serious injuries. Unfortunately, airbags are known to sometimes cause injuries and death not due to the forces of the collision itself.

Type IV Multiple impact collisions, rollover collisions, spinouts, etc., need to be reviewed and calculated carefully into the patients report. A detailed consultation, exam and probable X-ray images are warranted depending on other factors of the case.

Understanding the type(s) of collisions is critical in determining potential injuries. Typing implies the occupant is situated normally in their vehicle. Complex crashes may have multiple same or different types. All crash types should be listed in chronological order if all can be determined. For example, if an occupant is rear ended then

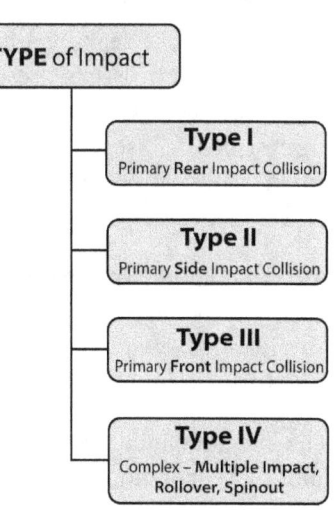

TYPE of Impact

Type I
Primary **Rear** Impact Collision

Type II
Primary **Side** Impact Collision

Type III
Primary **Front** Impact Collision

Type IV
Complex – Multiple Impact, Rollover, Spinout

---

75. Brian Henderson reveals the results of his extensive research into the impact of low-speed-change collisions *Personal Injury Law Journal* September 2006. (Brian Henderson the managing director of GBB Ltd Forensic Collision Investigation and Research)

76. *Whiplash-Associated Diseases* Rene Cailliet, MD. Dr. Calliet is a Professor Emeritus at the University Of Southern California School Of Medicine and a clinical professor at the Department of Physical Medicine Rehabilitation at the UCLA School of Medicine. Dr. Cailliet has written 17 texts on musculoskeletal problems that have sold more than 1.2 million copies. American Medical Association 2006

forced into a vehicle in front it would be a Type I – III. For additional information attend PersonalInjuryTrainingInstitute.com

Stages

Once injuries have occurred, the body tissues respond with inflammation and scar tissue. This process can continue in joints and soft tissue for up to 18 months following the initial injury. Scar tissue is formed through a cyclic pattern as was discussed in chapter three.

When inflammation occurs, chemicals from the body's white blood cells are released into the blood or affected tissues in an attempt to rid the body of foreign substances. This release of chemicals increases the blood flow to the area and may result in redness and warmth. Some of the chemicals cause leakage of fluid into the local tissues, resulting in swelling. Collagen fibers are formed as scar tissue. The inflammatory process may irritate nerves and cause pain.

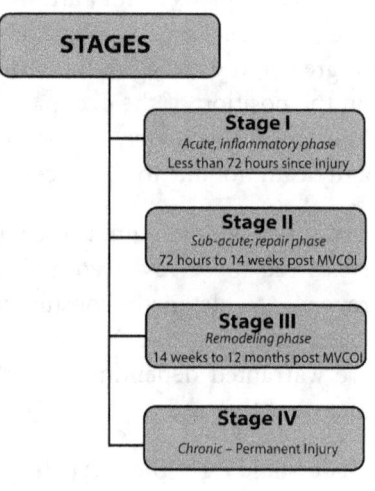

After the age of approximately fifteen years old, joints do not have the same blood supply or blood flow as muscles and bones. This physiological factor makes it more difficult for older bodies to heal joints and discs properly without medical/chiropractic intervention.

The increased number of cells and inflammatory substances within the joint cause irritation, wearing down of cartilage (cushions at the end of bones) and swelling of the joint lining. Excessive swelling causes pain. In micro-traumas the pain and swelling may be minimal at first. Eventually the swelling and scar formation become chronic, forming arthrofibrosis. This leads to increased pain and loss of function over time.

Arthrofibrosis is a complication that may occur within a damaged joint. The joint becomes inflamed and then fills up with internal scar tissue. As the scar tissue matures and tightens, the joint may become stiff. **If not treated early the stiffness may become permanent.**

For these reasons, it is important to know which stage of injury and recovery the patient is in to better formulate a treatment plan and predict the improvement or lack of improvement they are likely to experience.

Grades

The grading system of the Croft guidelines allows physicians to categorize a patient based objective evidence from exam, X-ray and if medically necessary other studies. This aids the doctor in building a road map of care by knowing the starting point of the patient. Furthermore, it gives an inter- and intra-professional communication platform that is easy to understand between doctors, attorneys, insurance companies, judges and juries.

Grades	Severity	Anatomical and Clinical Description
I	Minimal	No limitation of range of motion, no ligamentous injury, no neurological symptoms.
II	Slight	Limitation of range of motion, no ligamentous injury, no neurological findings.
III	Moderate	Limitation of range of motion, some ligamentous injury, neurological findings present.
IV	Moderate to Severe	Limitations of range of motion, ligamentous instability, neurological findings present, fracture or disc derangement
V	Severe	Requires surgical treatment and stabilization – chiropractic care post surgery.

With the calculated grade of injury in place combined with the years of research in human occupant injury and rehabilitation, we can apply the treatment recommendations. These recommendations are not a dictation of care. They do, however, offer an expected duration and number of visit outcome it typically takes most individuals with grade "x" injuries to maximize their recovery potential with chiropractic care, taking into account the patient's complicating factors.

Treatment Recommendation Based on Grade

Grades	Croft Frequency and Duration Guidelines						
	Daily	3x/wk	2x/wk	1x/wk	1x/m	Total Duration	Total Number of Visits
I	1 wk	1-2 wks	2-3 wks	4 wks		10 wks	21
II	1 wk	4 wks	4 wks	4 wks	4 mo	29 wks	33
III	1-2 wks	10 wks	10 wks	10 wks	6 mo	56 wks	76
IV	2-3 wks	16 wks	12 wks	20 wks	**	**	**
V	Surgical stabilzation necessary - Chiropractic care is post surgical.						

** May require permanent monthly or permanent palliative care

See "Research" on page 125 *for medical and chiropractic research from 1958 till present on treatment frequency and duration recommendations.*

Complicating Factors

There are a number of possibilities that can take place in any given MVC potentially but not necessarily adding to the complexity of injury and recovery. The following table might help explain why two individuals in the same vehicle in the same collision could sustain injuries requiring entirely different treatment and recovery times. Listed below are some complicating factors.

For a complete understanding of the affects these complicating factors have on patient recovery outcomes, it is recommended physicians attend a continuing education seminar offered by a specialist in the field of motor vehicle occupant injury recovery.

By combining a thorough patient history, a history of the MVC, a proper exam, and the necessary X-rays with the AMA and Penning trauma line measurements, doctors are able to more accurately diagnose problems. Following this initial diagnosis, physicians can use the Croft guidelines to categorize, grade and list any complicating factors the patient will have, giving the patient a more precise diagnosis and suggested treatment plan. With this information, a detailed report can be drafted. Proper reports create much clearer communication between doctors of different disciplines, the patient, the insurance companies and attorneys.

Listed below are some complicating risk factors.

Complicating Risk Factors (Preexisting)

- Advanced age (65+)
- Increased age (35-64)
- Metabolic disorders
- Congenital anomalies of the spine
- Developmental anomalies of the spine
- Degenerative disc disease
- Disc protrusion (HNP)
- Spondylosis
- Facet arthrosis
- Rheumatoid arthritis or other spinal arthritides
- Ankylosing spondylitis or other spondylarthropathy
- Scoliosis
- Prior spinal surgery
- Osteoporosis
- Prior vertebral fracture
- Paget's disease or other bone disease
- Spinal or foraminal stenosis
- Prior spinal injury
- Paraplegia or quadriplegia
- Fibromyalgia

Other Complicating Risk Factors

- Low Body Mass Index
- Premorbid arthritis
- Headache and/or neck pain and/or injury
- Front seat (vs. rear seat) position
- Non-failure of seat back
- Wet, damp, snowy or icy road conditions
- Impact by vehicle of greater mass
- Poor head restraint geometry/tall occupant
- Having the head turned at impact or side impact collision
- Use of seatbelt (shoulder harness)
- Out-of-position occupant (leaning forward/slumped, etc.)
- Rear impact collision (vs. other vectors)
- Crash speed under 10 mph
- Not adequately braced for impending impact
- Multiple Impact Collision
- Vehicle equipped with tow bar/hitch
- Airbag deployment
- Immediate onset of symptoms and/or neurological findings
- Initial back pain
- Greater number of initial symptoms
- Limited range of motion and/or neurological findings
- A loss of or reversal of the cervical lordotic curve
- Ligamentous instability
- Initial degenerative changes seen on radiographs
- Greater subjective cognitive impairment

Prognosis & Motor Vehicle Collision Occupant Injury Risk Factors:

By Jeffrey A. States DC

Motor vehicle collision occupant injury (MVCOI) prognostic research indicates that 39% to 56% of those injured in MVC's have persistent symptoms for years. [77] [78] [79] Early treatment is necessary for improve prognosis. Later treatment is medically necessary to address symptomatic exacerbations following Maximum Medical Improvement (MMI).[80]

There are a number of crash dynamics and occupant kinematics known to potentially cause injuries in motor vehicle collisions (MVC). These are known as motor vehicle collision occupant injury risk factors (MVCOIRF). While this topic can be highly complex and detailed with numerous areas to discuss and understand, in this text I will keep it on a more simple level.

---

77. Macnab I: Acceleration injuries of the cervical spine J Bone Joint Surg 46A(8):1797–1799, 1964

78. Norris SH, Watt I: The prognosis of neck injuries resulting from rear-end vehicle collisions. J Bone Joint Surg 65B(5):608–611,1983

79. There are many papers on MVCOI prognosis a good summary is found in the Whiplash Poster Book, specifically Prognosis from SRISD

80. "The point at which a condition has stabilized and is unlikely to change (improve or worsen) substantially in the next year with or without treatment. American Medical Associations Guides to the Evaluation of Permanent Impairment 6th Edition. p 612

Fundamentally, how do we know that MVCOIRFs exists? Occupants have been receiving injuries from car crashes for more than a century. There have been injury patterns that have developed over this time. Car crash researchers at all levels understand most of these risk factors. Since car crash researchers never design or crash cars to cause occupant injuries, it behooves them to know what will likely injure occupants. This way certain MVCOIRF's can be eliminated when possible. This of course does not mean that human volunteers involved in these test crashes have never been injured. Unfortunately, all too often volunteers have been injured, even in lower energy collisions as low as 2.5 mph. Since car crash research is not specifically designed to find injuries, the area of properly determining volunteer injuries is commonly ignored. For this reason I have been vocal for many years against human crash testing. There should never, ever be any more live human volunteer car crash testing/research (at any speed).

For example in 1999 I attended my first day of car crash testing. One of the female volunteers arrived to the crash site with very long hair up in a bun on the back of her head. This created increased distance between her head and the head restraint (HR) when seated in the target vehicle. This alone is an increased MVCOI risk factor. The further the head is from the front of the head restraint the greater the potential for occupant injury. The volunteer was asked to make a ponytail to the right side of her head. This allowed a more compliant head to head restraint geometry, getting her head within inches to the HR at impact from the rear.

Another way that we know about MVCOIRFs is volumes of car crash research and collected data from around the world. This includes treating physician offices that see injured occupants. Quite frankly with the correct form of history patterns are clear of what is more likely to hurt occupants. Because of these facts good treating doctors will ask the correct questions and document findings within their records and reports. It is my opinion that each of these recognized risk factors are discovered in each person injury (PI) case.

MVCOIRF's are dynamic aspects known in collision, medical and scientific literature that increases the potential for injury in the car collisions. These MVCOIRF's have been reported and validated in this literature. When these factors are present in a real crash, the risk of injury is increased. Needless to say, the risk of poor outcome is also increased. Multiple risk factors, of course, increase the potential for poorer outcome.

The risks of injury in MVC's range from 39–59% statistically, as reported in a number of publications spanning more than six decades. According to Dr. Croft, a CAD expert and author, "the risk of injury has been reported variously, but the overall risk is thought to be about 50%. Thus, out of a hundred persons subjected to such collisions, about half of those injured will recover, while the other half will develop some degree of chronic pain and/or dysfunction." [81]

These known MVC injury risk factors have been evaluated in MVC's with human and dummy research. In certain crashes risks factors are eliminated and compared to collisions where the factors were not eliminated. Using scientific instruments to measure forces to the humans and dummies it is clear when certain risks factors are eliminated occupant forces are reduced which leads to the reduction of injury potential.

The following is a list of specific MVCOIR's, which a MVC occupant may experience. These are known in whiplash scientific literature that contribute or lead to a poor outcome:

- Increasing age i.e., middle age (35 years old or more)
- Female gender and/or Low Body Mass Index
- Premorbid arthritis and/or headaches and/ or neck pain and/or injury
- Front seat (vs. rear seat) position
- Non-failure of seat back
- Impact by vehicle of greater mass
- Wet, Damp, Snowy or Icy road conditions
- Poor head restraint geometry and/or tall occupant
- Having the head turned at impact or side impact collision
- Use of seatbelt /shoulder harness. (Always wear your seatbelt. It could save your life.)
- Out of position occupant (leaning forward, slumped, etc)

---

81. The Whiplash Poster System 2nd Edition Arthur C. Croft p20

- Rear impact collision (vs. other vectors)
- Crash speed under 10 mph
- Not adequately braced for impending impact
- Multiple impact collision
- Vehicle equipped with tow bar/hitch
- Airbag deployment
- Immediate onset of symptoms and/or severe symptoms
- Initial back pain
- Greater number of initial symptoms
- Limited range of motion and/or neurological findings
- A loss of, or reversal of the cervical lordotic curve
- Ligamentous instability
- Initial degenerative changes seen on radiographs
- Greater subjective cognitive impairment
- Interior vehicle collisions

There is no grading scale that assigns significance or value to each MVCOIRF. Clearly some risk factors are more dangerous than others. Still other MVCOIRF's have a higher injury potential than others.

The highest risk factors are listed here:

- Female gender
- Surprised by impact, not adequately braced for impact
- Poor head restraint geometry [82]
- Having the head turned at impact or side impact collision
- Use of seatbelt /shoulder harness. [83] (Always wear your seatbelt. It could save your life.)
- Rear impact collision (vs. other vectors)
- Multiple impact collision
- Interior vehicle collisions

---

82. Type I collisions
83. Type I collisions

There may be other MVCOIRF's discovered in a specific PI case. If found, treating physicians should list them in the patients report. The greater the number of MVCOIRF's, the greater the potential for occupant injuries. Statistically about 50% of occupants in MVC's are injured. If an occupant is injured in a MVC, however other occupant(s), also in the crash states they were not injured, why be surprised. Perfect statistics, one injured, one uninjured. Just because one is exposed to a risk does not equal injury. Perhaps the uninjured asks to be checked out by a physician. The doctor does not find any cervical acceleration/deceleration (CAD) or MVCOI's or any associated crash symptoms. The physical examination is normal, no medical necessity for further testing. Basically, this individual in the crash is not injured. Now the real questions:

- One is injured? Yes
- One is not injured? Yes
- They were both in the same crash? Yes
- They both received the same forces? No
- They both have the same MVCOIRF's? No (Some MVCOIRF may be the same, some not the same.)

In cases where one occupant is clearly injured and another is not, I suggest physicians meet with the uninjured occupant(s) if possible. Take a brief history specific to crash dynamics to determine specific MVCOIRF's of this occupant. I have done this countless time over my career. I discovered without question the injured occupant has significantly more MVCOIRF's than the uninjured occupant. Certainly regarding the injured patient there were enough MVCOIRF's from the impact to produce injuries. While in the same crash the uninjured occupant only has a few MVCOIRF's.

One can never determine that because someone is not injured in a collision that other occupants should not be injured. Occupants can have MVCOIRF's particular to them. Look at each occupant, discover their crash dynamics and human kinematics can then leads toward determining MVCOIRF's specific to that individual.

Working Together for Healing and Justice

Croft Guidelines for Diagnosis and Treatment of Whiplash Injuries

By Dr. Jeffrey A. States

The Croft Guidelines (CG) are specifically for whiplash or better defined as Cervical Acceleration Deceleration (CAD) injuries in Personal Injury (PI) and Workers Compensation cases. CG are to be used by chiropractic physicians in **diagnosing** and **treating motor vehicle collision occupant injuries (MVCOI) with CAD's**.

The CG grading system is specifically for the diagnosis and Chiropractic treatment of whiplash or CAD injuries. Treatment protocols for cases involving whiplash injuries are included with these guidelines following grading. Dr. Art Croft, an internationally known chiropractic physician, whiplash researcher, lecturer and author, developed this CAD guideline. Croft published his first work in 1993 in American Chiropractic Association Journal and later in 1995 in the text Whiplash Injuries. Foreman & Croft published more current information in Whiplash Injuries 2001 third edition[84] on page 61 Table 1-14. In the early 90's I summarized the CG in an efficient singular page. It is available free on our web site and attached to this article.

Utah Chiropractic Physicians Association was the first chiropractic association in the nation to approve the CGs. This move followed the Oklahoma Board of Chiropractic Examiners approval.[85] I have personally assisted several states in understanding and considering or passing the CG's. Now many states and at least one Canadian providence have adopted these CG's. Currently the CG's are the most used United States national standards for CAD care by doctors of chiropractic. Since 1993 many Utah chiropractic physicians have used

---

84. 2002

85. For more details and information see http://www.ok.gov/chiropracticboard/documents/The Croft Whiplash Management Guidelines Endorsed by the OBCE.pdf

the CGs in CAD cases. Further, since the early 90's doctors have been submitting these standards with their reports to automobile insurance companies for motor vehicle collision occupant injuries (MVCOI) cases involving whiplash injuries.

The bottom line is with these standards, individuals with CAD injuries due to motor vehicle collisions (MVC) can receive better care attempting to return to pre-crash physical state. Automobile insurance companies (including workers compensation carriers) using unacceptable standards can be challenged since they are not adhering to accepted national researched protocols.

Some auto carriers hire unscrupulous doctors to perform unethical paper reviews and questionable defense medical examinations. Some of the problems noted with these doctors have been making up their own substandard chiropractic care guidelines and erroneously quoting Mercy Guidelines, AMA Impairment Guides, and Agency for Health Care Policy and Research. None of these publications have anything to do with chiropractic care in CAD cases, let alone have any support from the UCPA.

States adopting the Croft standards take a major step forward in diagnostic and care guidelines for CAD victims. These standards and grading systems have been taught across the nation for years. It is the responsibility of every chiropractic physicians caring for individuals with whiplash to intimately know and understand how to properly grade CAD cases in accordance with these treatment standards. If you need to know how to use these standards contact https://personalinjurytraininginstitute.com/ email PI questions to pitiinfo@gmail.com, or http://www.chiro.org/LINKS/croft.shtml for more information.

A few doctors will attempt to take advantage of the system. The CG's are not blank checks for insurance payments regarding CAD treatments. As taught by Personal Injury Training Institute and Dr. Croft, these protocols are not prescriptions for care nor do they provide for dishonest abuses of medically unnecessary treatment. In addition, other established chiropractic care guidelines and standards should be used to complement treatment protocols for non-CAD diagnosis. On the other hand, certain cases may require more care than protocols indicate due to underlying conditions or MVCOI complications as published.

Chiropractic physicians have amazing skills and techniques to help patients with CAD injuries. Physicians providing excellent care may find their treatment visit numbers are below the numbers found in the CG. I encourage you to continue to provide excellent care with the highest standards with the utmost credibility.

Croft Guidelines Pros and Cons

Croft guidelines (CG) are standards that take a major step forward in diagnostic care for whiplash or cervical acceleration/deceleration (CAD) victims treated by chiropractic physicians. I have written down a few of the pros and cons of these Croft Guidelines

The Croft Guideline Pros:

- Assist individuals with CAD injuries due to MVCOI to receive appropriate care by chiropractic physicians.
- Allow those injured in Motor Vehicle Collisions an accurate CAD diagnosis that leads to reasonable treatment parameters.
- Automobile insurance companies using unacceptable standards can be challenged when not adhering to approved and researched CAD protocols.
- Allows Chiropractic Physicians to determine CAD standards versus alleged unsubstantiated individuals or rogue chiropractors treatment opinions.

The Croft Guideline Cons:

- There may be a few doctors who will attempt to take advantage of the system, dishonest abuses of medically unnecessary treatment.
- Certain atypical CAD cases may require greater care than protocols indicate due to underlying conditions or complications.
- Limited to Cervical spine/CAD injuries.

This is an attempt to summarize some of the known benefits and problems with the CG's. This summary is not designed to fully educate the details of the CG's. Please see my summary of the CG listed below.

Dr. Jeffrey A. States maintains a second opinion/impairment rating practice and is the main speaker for Personal Injury Training Institute.

He believes there are volumes of information available regarding MVCOIs provided by the best educators in this field including Murphy, Croft and Nordoff. Personal Injury Training Institute is not another information disseminating company. It is a problem solving training that teaches tried and true methods for helping physicians and attorneys work together to assist individuals with MVCOI's. For more information visit https://personalinjurytraininginstitute.com/. Our PI trainings series is available online. Visit our website for a practical usable summary of the Croft Guidelines.

When, Where and Why to Refer Auto Accident Patients

Physicians

Following a motor vehicle collision, occupants might see a variety of physicians or therapists. High-speed collisions typically result in injuries requiring some type of emergency care. Even low-speed collisions often require limited medical intervention; however, many occupants do not realize the extent of their injuries until days, weeks or months later. Whiplash and soft tissue injuries can present symptoms anytime from the day of the injury up to two years post-trauma.

When looking at the research for treatment protocols, frequency, and duration of patient injury rehabilitation care there are referral patterns that must be followed. Without interdisciplinary co-care or by not following these research based treatment suggestions many patients will have difficulty reaching a true maximum medical improvement or will develop a late onset chronic problem stemming from their MVC injuries.

TESTIMONIAL:

I had neck & upper back pain due to a car accident. I was so tight that I would suffer muscles spasms in my ribs.

After Hours/Urgent Care recommended I see a Certified Auto Accident Chiropractor.

The Doctor listened to me, took X-rays, went over in detail with me the findings and talked about treatment.

I received step-by-step instructions of each process and treatments ranged from adjustments and massage to stretching and exercises.

I have improved and feel better than prior to my treatments.

At least check it out for yourself. It could help you gain the ability to do things without pain!

~Leslie

First Response

High speed MVCs characteristically result in the more gruesome and visible injuries. Occupant or witnesses typically call for police and ambulance support. Emergency medical technicians (EMT) are trained to provide pre-hospital emergency medical services. This may include assessing a patient's condition, performing such emergency medical procedures as are needed to maintain a patient airway with adequate breathing and cardiovascular circulation until the patient can be transferred to an appropriate destination for advanced medical care. Their skills of intervention include controlling severe external bleeding, treating shock, cardiopulmonary resuscitation, defibrillation, body immobilization to prevent spinal damage, and splinting of bone fractures.

Emergency Room

In cases where the trauma and injuries from the MVC are severe, the first response team will transport patients via ambulance or air-transport to an emergency room. Emergency room physicians and staff are primarily trained to assess, treat, and stabilize injury. When necessary, patients are admitted to the hospital. In such cases the patient is transferred to a physician specializing in a given area.

Patients with less severe cases are given home instructions and are released. Rarely are these patients referred to "outside" specialists. Typically it is suggested that if they have any further problems they should see their general practitioner, or they are given a prescription for non-steroidal anti-inflammatory drugs, antidepressants and/or muscle relaxants as suggested in the National Institute of Neurological Disorder Guidelines referenced earlier.

> **TESTIMONIAL:**
>
> I was in a car accident and had neck pain and bad headaches.
>
> My husband and others had referred me to the chiropractor (a specialist).
>
> I went to a very informative workshop and received instruction during procedures, massage therapy, weight training (Physical Therapy) and adjustments.
>
> Definitely give chiropractic a go! I feel so much better and I hold my head up straighter—my posture has improved.
>
> ~Angela

Instacare/Urgent Care/After Hours Medical

These are local clinics offering a cross between emergency room and general practitioner services. Their popularity is growing in suburbs and rural areas as they are convenient, personable and much less expensive than an emergency room visit. These facilities might see patients after they have been released from the ER but are not feeling any improvement or patients who did not sustain life threatening injuries and opted not to go to the ER after the accident. Most likely these physicians prescribe something similar to the National Institute of Neurological Disorders Guidelines as well.

It is important to note that modern trauma care in the U.S. is outstanding. America has the most advanced trauma and emergency care in the world. It is the lack of communication or reluctance to refer the "less than life threatening" cases that ultimately result in the unacceptably high statistics of chronic problems following a motor vehicle collision.

Chiropractic Physicians

According to the Journal of Orthopedic Medicine, "Chiropractic is the only proven effective treatment in chronic [whiplash] cases." [86] Early intervention drastically increases the effectiveness.

Doctors of chiropractic are skilled physicians trained in the function and rehabilitation of the neuro-muscular-skeletal system. Doctors of chiropractic, like medical doctors, can choose an area of specialty following their general training. A medical doctor may choose to specialize in pediatrics, orthopedics, pulmonary surgery, etc. A chiropractic physician may choose to train or certify in sports injuries, chiropractic pediatrics, motor vehicle injury rehabilitation, or other specialized areas.

Any physician, including a chiropractic physician, is licensed to treat motor vehicle collision occupant injuries (MVCOI). However, the treatment protocols, interdisciplinary communication, and documentation performed by a chiropractic physician certified in the treatment of MVC injuries, is more detailed than the average chiropractic physician.

---

86. A symptomatic classification of whiplash injury and the implications for treatment, The Journal of Orthopaedic Medicine- Volume 21(I), 1999, pages 22–25

A doctor of chiropractic specializing in MVCOI is a key component in successful recovery and even litigation cases for several reasons.

First of all, patients who follow chiropractic physician prescription of treatment within the Croft Guidelines maximize healing potential. This careful and informed treatment has an additional benefit in that it makes the chiropractic physician a strong expert witness in litigation if he/she has been communicating with the other physicians throughout the course of care.

Chiropractic treatments often help in the following areas:

> **TESTIMONIAL:**
>
> After a car accident I had constant low back pain. I had tried Physical Therapy but with minimal results.
>
> My Chiropractor did a "Hands-on" examination and began treatment with adjustments, ice, e-stim, exercises and traction that together were very effective.
>
> I have had considerable low back pain relief as I have continued treatments.
>
> Don't knock it till you try it! Continue your treatments then decide - I love the results I am getting!
>
> ~Mark

- Reduction of intersegmental swelling or joint swelling
- Restoration of mobility and range of motion of fixated joints
- Reduction of spinal joint swelling which removes unwanted pressure on nerves thus restoring nervous system function, reducing pain
- Reduction in the formation of unwanted scar tissue (arthrofibrosis) that often leads to chronic pain and symptoms
- Council or prescription relating to nutrition for healing (anti-inflammatory foods and herbs)
- Offering limited physical rehabilitation, physio therapies and massage
- Offering passive treatment to reduce pain preparing the patient to better handle active treatments of physical therapy often needed for rehabilitation to a full recovery

With patients who plateau prematurely or prior to an expected maximal medical improvement, there are other options. (S) A small number of the more difficult cases may qualify for manipulation under anesthesia (MUA). MUA is a procedure often used by orthopedic physicians to set broken bone or align "subluxated joints," Chiropractic physicians who are trained and certified in this area can work with medical doctors who are also trained in MUA. Together with an anesthesiologist, this team approach has shown incredibly positive results, helping tough cases to break through the plateau, find relief and avoid surgery.

Physical Therapists

Early intervention with physical therapy can be very helpful. As with chiropractic care, the earlier the patient is seen following a MVC, the less permanent scar tissue will form. Physical therapist Brian Rodriguez stated, "I have never seen chiropractic care worsen a physical therapy case. After a month, there is already scar tissue where their case becomes progressively more difficult to yield the same results. For this reason, patients typically do better when treated early."

Chiropractic and physical therapy complement each other by increasing range of motion and reducing pain. With early intervention physical therapy may be more painful than starting later, but modalities can be altered to ease the patient toward a better recovery

Physical therapy for whiplash associated disorders is very comprehensive and focuses on several key areas:

- Decreasing pain and other symptoms associated with the injury
- Restoring soft-tissue and joint mobility to achieve full range of motion
- Improving muscular strength and endurance through individualized exercise programs
- Educating patients regarding the nature of the injury and guidance in managing symptoms and enhancing recovery

Rodriguez points out, "Physical therapists thoroughly evaluate each patient and design an individualized treatment plan which may include manual therapy (hands-on techniques), corrective exercises to restore strength, flexibility, endurance and stability, modalities (heat, ice, electrical stimulation etc.), mechanical traction, home exercise instruction, posture training, self-help tips etc.

Research shows that a proper physical therapy program including manual therapy and exercise effectively reduces pain and headaches, increases mobility and restores function."

Licensed Massage Therapist

Massage therapy can play an important role in flushing out the chemical by-products of inflammation in soft tissues thereby reducing swelling and pain while restoring some range of motion. Depending on the severity of the injuries, massage or various types of massage may be utilized in the course of care and patient recovery. Some massage techniques listed from least aggressive to more aggressive might include (but are not limited to): ice massage, effleurage, nimmo trigger-point technique, rolfing and active release technique.

These techniques help:

- Reduce inflammation in the muscles
- Flush out chemical byproducts of inflammation that are nerve irritants and cause pain
- Restore mobility
- Relieve pain

Orthopedic Surgeon

Surgeons agree that surgery should be a last resort. There are numerous reasons an individual might need surgery following injuries sustained in a MVC. These are not limited to spinal disc herniation. It is common to see hand and arm injuries from airbag deployment, shoulder injuries from seatbelts, and lower extremity injuries from the foot placement at the time of impact. A referral to an orthopedic surgeon from a primary care physician is warranted in a MVC case where the patient's injuries are severe or non-responsive to conservative care after 6 weeks. A referral to an orthopedic surgeon is just that: a referral. The surgeon may have other suggestions to offer prior to the need for surgery.

Patients who have reached a plateau in their progress without reaching their full recovery potential (MMI) and are not automatic candidates for surgery, they may benefit greatly from manipulation under anesthesia.

Spine Specialist

This is a term often used referring to an orthopedic surgeon who specializes in the spine. It is important to be clear with patients when referring to a "spine specialist" since doctors of chiropractic are also spine specialists. It also is important to help distinguish the patient needs and send them to the appropriate specialist for their stage of recovery. If they are presenting signs and symptoms suspect of spinal injury such as foot drop, muscle weakness and atrophy in the extremities, lack of bowel and bladder control, etc., then a surgical consult is definitely in order. Otherwise, the spinal specialist they should be seeing is a chiropractic physician. Chiropractic is not alternative care, especially in the auto collision arena.[87][88] Chiropractic physicians are the preferred and logical choice of care for traumatic injuries of this nature.

Psychologist

According to psychologist Victoria Burgess, it is sound advice to have victims of traumatic MVCs receive a psychiatric evaluation. "Most general practitioners and even social workers lack the psychiatric training to properly evaluate. Only psychologists (not psychiatrists) do actual testing." She goes on to say, psychologists are able to perform a psychiatric evaluation test that is 85% accurate in documenting the extent of mental trauma the patient has experienced and to what extent it has affected their functional capacity. This is helpful in determining not only the severity and mental trauma sustained by an individual involved in a MVC but detecting if someone is playing up their symptoms for personal or financial gain. For these reasons, a psychiatric evaluation might be more important than most physicians realize."

Other Specialist

There are a number of other specialists that might be involved in a motor vehicle occupant injury case, including TMJ specialists, physiatrists and pain clinics. Pain clinics are by design an 'end of care' model. They are intended to help patients who have tried everything else and still suffer with unbearable pain. Many of these patients are bordering on an addiction to medication. Unfortunately, the vast majority of MVC patients suffering in this manner have not tried the proper channels of rehabilitation following their crash. In other words, they only tried medication to control the pain following their injury rather than seeking out the physical medicines: chiropractic, physical

---

87. Chiropractic treatment of chronic 'whiplash' injuries Injury Volume 27, Issue 9, November 1996, pages 643–645

88. A symptomatic classification of whiplash injury and the implications for treatment; The Journal of Orthopedic Medicine: Volume 21(I), 1999, pages 22–25

therapy, massage. Today's avant-garde pain clinics offer these services combined with their medical physician who can help properly manage the patients' medications.

Impairment Ratings/Reports

Decades if MVCOI statistics prove that approximately 40–60% of those injured will have symptoms for years. This also means that many get better. Unfortunately, for a multitude of reasons, but primarily due to the magnitude of MVCOIs, small percentages are left with permanent symptoms and chronic conditions. Once these individual reach a permanent and stationary status, meaning not getting significantly better or worse they may qualify for a permanent impairment rating. Quality impairment ratings from a non-treating physician may also provide excellent second opinions.

Different governments and systems may use different standards for impairment ratings. For example, on the job injuries may have specific impairment guides to follow for worker injuries. The international standard for impairment ratings has the American Medical Association's *Guides to the Evaluation of Permanent Impairment*. At the time of this publication the 6th Edition is the current standard for most of the United States.

Just like other areas of specialty in the chiropractic profession, some physicians are highly trained in impairment ratings. Some trainings are limited to covering impairment to the spine and extremities, while others trainings cover the whole body. Impairment ratings attempts to assist the multitude of professions working in PI to better communicate. For example healthcare, insurance, and legal industries do not speak the same languages. To assist in understanding the magnitude of occupant residual injuries, impairment-rating systems have been developed over the last 50 decades.

Injured occupants who are left with residual symptoms and conditions may qualify for a permanent impairment. Impairments are not just for MVCOIs; they can be used in many different forums, but are usually used for traumatized or diseased individuals. If someone is perfectly healthy with normal function they have 0% whole person impairment. If someone is dead they have 100% impairment. The following is an example to assist in understanding the impairment principles. Of course, there are many details and steps to obtain and impairment that are not listed.

Simply put, if a patient has the following diagnosis:

- Type I, Grade IV, Stage IV late traumatic cervical acceleration/deceleration injuries (CAD),
- Complicated by post CAD traumatic cervicogenic headaches,
- How bad is this condition?
- What are these conditions worth?

Since insurance employees and legal workers are not trained in healthcare, the above diagnosis is not of much value. On the other hand, if the report listed this patient's impairment as three percent whole person impairment, meaning this patient has lost three percent of their health and function, all parties have an idea of how bad this problem is.

Physicians and personal injury attorneys should receive substantial additional training in impairment ratings if they are involved with MVCOIs.

Disability Report

For an even fewer number of patients who continue to struggle, a disability report will be needed for their case. This is typically performed by a physician or physical therapist trained in disability ratings. The report, which takes significant time to generate, will help paint a picture of the limitations an individual may experience for the remainder of their life. It compares post-trauma limitations to their pre-injury status on range of motion, activity levels and lifting ability. It calculates how this will affect their work and income potential, sex life, family life and overall quality of life. This is a valuable tool for attorneys to use in litigation. A disability report is necessary in only a small number of cases as compared to the vast number of MVCs that take place each year. Ideally, this type of report is avoidable by patients and physicians working together following the recommendations provided in this book.

Attorneys

The insurance industry has become more share holder focused and less client need focused in the recent decades. Some insurance companies remain ethical and balance business with client protection. Globally speaking, however, the industry has become very skilled at making it difficult for medical bills and restitution to be paid to clients who have suffered a loss. For this and other reasons it is sound advice to consult an attorney specializing in personal injury work as soon as possible following a motor vehicle collision.

Personal Injury Attorneys

by Bryan Larson, Esq.

Personal Injury Health Care:

In the years that I have practiced law, I have taught many seminars to both lawyers and physicians concerning the subject of personal injury cases and health care. I have often been asked the question, "What is the difference between personal injury healthcare and 'regular' healthcare?" In other words, how does the fact that a patient has been involved in a trauma event cause needed health care practices to be different? When the patient is involved in a compensation-seeking claim, does it change the requirements for medical documentation? The short answer is that in a perfect world there would be no difference. However, in reality, ordinary office visits usually have the patient making a series of subjective complaints, with a physician acting on auto-pilot with a standard set of well-known remedies to solve a "routine" set of symptoms. In this situation, SOAP notes are scant, examinations are bare bones or incomplete and subsequent reports to insurance adjusters or attorneys are infrequent or nonexistent. However, in recent years, the paperwork demands and pressures on the health care industry have increased to such a point that the gap between ordinary health care and forensic health care has narrowed. Nevertheless, the perception is that personal injury health care is more burdensome in terms of documentation.

Personal injury or forensic health care demands documentation, objectification, and justification for every modality administered. In no other arena will the physician's work be more scrutinized and challenged than in the personal injury arena. Insurance companies are constantly looking for reasons to not pay a claim. Juries are told that they must only award the cost of medical care that is "reasonable, necessary, and arises out of the subject incident." Accordingly, if an insurance company can find a reason for non-payment they think they can "sell" to a jury, the health care provider may not get paid.

What is reasonable? What is necessary? What is caused by, aggravated by, or related to the subject incident? Each of these three questions poses fertile ground for defense attorneys to challenge and question the health care that was provided. If the defense is successful in convincing the jury that something was not reasonable or necessary, or was unrelated to the subject incident, then the judge tells the jury that the subject medical care cannot be awarded as damages to the victim. Under this standard, insurance adjusters, long before trial, determine whether or not they will voluntarily choose to pay the claim.

Should physicians be concerned whether the cost of their care is awarded as damages to the patient? Yes! This is obvious if the physician is working on a lien basis or has agreed to wait until the patient receives his or her settlement or judgment before the bill is collected. However, it is also important because even if the physician is not directly a recipient of the jury's decision, the physician has probably already been paid for his or her services by virtue of an insurance policy which has a direct interest in subrogation or reimbursement in the outcome of the claim. Personal Injury Protection or No-Fault benefits in Utah or other No-fault states (or "med-pay" benefits as is often provided in other non-no-fault states) generally has a direct right of reimbursement. Likewise, health care insurers have a right of reimbursement under the ERISA law which is also directly affected by the outcome of the jury's decision. If for some reason the amount of medical care or chiropractic care is not awarded by the jury, then the health care insurer is not reimbursed. Failure to reimburse the health care insurer for payments expended on behalf of the patient further pushes up the cost of insurance making health care less affordable for all. Insurance companies are also beginning to seek restitution from health care providers they previously paid where a court has subsequently determined such payment was inappropriate.

In a personal injury or forensic healthcare situation, the physician's records will be read and reviewed in detail by attorneys for both sides. The insurance company, the judge and jury (if the matter goes to trial) will also review the records. The plaintiff's attorney utilizes the physician's records to determine what kind of case the plaintiff really has and whether it is even worth pursuing. How badly injured an individual is and how much those injuries directly relate to the claim has a direct bearing on the size of the case and the plaintiff attorney's evaluation. It is not the only factor, but it is probably the most important factor.

Some may be surprised by the previous sentence. How could the extent of the plaintiff's injuries not be the only factor in determining the value of the plaintiff's case? There are numerous other factors also influential in that determination. The strength of the plaintiff's case is also controlled by the strength of the plaintiff as a witness, the strength of the defendant as a witness, the facts related to causation of the accident, issues of comparative negligence, if any, the strength of the physician as a witness, juror bias, the nature of the negligence or "badness" of the act involved and of course the relative strength of the attorneys involved representing the parties. This last factor is generally far less important than it is made out to be on television or in the media since jurors try to ignore any lawyer and discount what they say if possible. All of these factors, and others, work in concert to determine what decision a jury might make, and accordingly, the relative evaluation of the case by both parties. In a typical simple negligence case (whether it be a slip-and-fall, automobile accident, or professional negligence), it is possible for the defendant to be responsible for the injuries but for the jury to determine that the injuries are not very big or that the health care provider was not useful and unimportant to the patient's outcome. If either of these scenarios occur, the jury's verdict could be minuscule or non-existent. If that occurs, the plaintiff and the plaintiff's attorney will have exhausted thousands of dollars in both money and time in an unprofitable endeavor. Juries are ordered by the court to award money only for compensation for the wrong and not to award money for punishment of the wrongdoer. Only in very rare circumstances does the court allow something called "punitive damages" which provides for the punishment of the defendant.

In the process of making their determination, juries are extremely skeptical. Jurors are instructed by the court that they cannot make any decision until convinced by a preponderance of the evidence that a certain outcome is justified. The attitude of jurors in recent years has been to come to the courthouse suspicious of the system, suspicious of the lawyers, and suspicious of anyone claiming to be injured and asking for money. Jurors have been preached to by the insurance industry for decades about how there are too many lawsuits, too many lawyers, too many people trying to sue someone simply to milk the system and get something for nothing. Political parties have often used the alleged "run-away court system" as justification for their political agendas to pass various versions of "tort reform" to take away the rights of injured persons to seek fair compensation. The news media has presented the extra-ordinary and absurd case that occasionally happens with outcomes that, to the casual listener, seem to be evidence of a judicial system that has run amuck. In most of these cases, the media has also not told the "other side of the story" and explained why a jury of citizens, after having heard all of the evidence, will make such a determination. The average person on the street believes that jury verdicts are simply too high. When they are given an opportunity to sit on a jury, people come in to the courtroom with a pre-conceived notion that they must see to it that fewer dollars are awarded. These prospective jurors are also consumers tired of the high cost of everything, including and especially health care. It is into this environment that the plaintiff and his counsel try to persuade the jury that the case before them is different and is meritorious and not frivolous. It is because of these special burdens that the treating physician needs to understand that gone are the days when anything that a physician says will be believed and accepted as true. Gone are the days when any old documentation or note taking a physician tries to scribble on paper will be accepted as gospel. Likewise, gone are the days when simply anything the physician does for the patient will be considered valuable and any charge the physician makes will be considered reasonable. It is in this environment that the physician must document his records so that the records standing alone, when reviewed by the jurors in the jury room, will tell them everything that needs to be shared about condition of the patient and the treatment given by the physician, its justification and the value of the charges. Even if the physician is called to covet to testify (which is increasingly rare), the physician's verbal explanation of what he or she did to the patient is often not enough to persuade the jury. A jury tends to discount the verbal testimony of witnesses and instead relies far more heavily on the black and white documentation proof before them in the jury room. In short, if the physician's records are not up to par, his verbal testimony will be discounted or ignored and the charges for the physician's care will be denied.

Examination

Effective personal injury health care begins with the physician's initial examination. The examination needs to be thorough and complete, with a complete patient history and checking all body systems and functions. The patient's history will often reveal data essential to injury causation and apportionment issues. It is hard to know where to send a patient if you do not know where he has been.

One common problem with emergency rooms is that they are only concerned with things that are an immediate emergency. If the person has no broken bones, is not bleeding and is breathing, the patient is generally discharged from the emergency room within a few hours with a hefty bill and only minimal instructions to seek follow-up care.

American society has long placed health care providers on an imaginary pinnacle of wisdom and influence such that most people will do nothing about their health care unless they are told to do so by a doctor. If the doctor does not give them explicit instructions for follow-up care, many individuals do not seek it until injuries have developed and manifest in such ways that they become impossible to avoid. Emergency rooms in this country are overburdened and overrun. Likewise, there is also no question that emergency rooms are simply not set up to micromanage patient healthcare. They are triage facilities designed only to provide initial screening of the most serious injuries to allow other health care providers to provide the rest of the needed care. Unfortunately, many ER facilities counsel patients that soft tissue injuries will simply spontaneously resolve without further care. This advice leads to both unnecessary patient suffering and often further complications with improper healing.

Unfortunately, many chiropractic physicians and MD's in private practice tend to only examine and focus on those areas of the body that they are most familiar with and comfortable treating. For example, chiropractors who ordinarily focus on the spine oftentimes overlook symptoms related to the extremities. This initial oversight can allow problems to develop that could have been corrected early. However, when the problems do develop later, the record makes the problem look like they were new problems. A more thorough patient history could have laid the foundation to build a bridge to the developing problems. But, if the record is silent, the insurance industry will challenge the "new" symptoms as being unrelated to the subject traumatic event. Failure to include an undiagnosed component may cause the treating physicians treatment plan to go down the wrong path. This is also inefficient and unproductive for the patient. Furthermore, in front of a jury, it can make it look like a physician was careless and incomplete in his or her work. This problem is complicated by the fact that often, when a patient has a pantheon of symptoms, the greater symptoms and pain can often mask the lesser symptoms. Although it is best to prioritize treatment to address the greater problems first, this should never be used as an excuse for ignoring the lesser problems. All problems should be diagnosed and addressed in a systematic way. The patient's complete initial history and detailed description of the accident can reveal much for the physician and prevent the "overlooking" of problems.

Once the initial thorough examination and all diagnostic studies have been completed, a complete and thorough diagnosis should be rendered. To the extent that this diagnosis can be graded in terms of degrees, it should be done so that the diagnosis taken at the outset of care can be further used as a baseline both for the improvement of the patient's condition and also a baseline in the event there are subsequent traumatic events which the insurance industry will try to use as an explanation for the patient's problems. For chiropractors, the Croft Guidelines are excellent at doing this. They allow a system of grading and typing the injury in such a way that can be subsequently compared as time passes and new events occur. Furthermore, the Croft Guidelines provide exceptional researched and accepted treatment protocols for care of the patient. They are easy to defend.

In short, measuring the patient's condition gives you a place to start when measuring the patient's improvement through the course of care. Without documented and measured improvement, the care given will be challenged as being merely palliative and unnecessary. If it is unnecessary, it will not be paid for.

Once an appropriate diagnosis is reached and care has begun, care should be continued only as long as progress is occurring as demonstrated through objectified and measured re-examination. Re-examination should occur at consistent intervals during the course of care. In the chiropractic model of treatment, I recommend once every twelve visits or once every thirty days. In no event should a re-examination occur later than six weeks after beginning care. If the patient's condition is not improving, do something different. Change modalities, try something new, or refer the patient out. If you continue to treat the patient when no progress is being measured, you run a high risk that you will be working for free. Not even the finest legal counsel can guarantee that you will recover your fees and charges if the attorney cannot prove that what you did provided a clear value to the patient. Furthermore, at the end of care, the patient will not only be frustrated and angry at the physician, but he will probably tell his friends. The most valuable patient is the one who refers others to the practice. Leave your patients satisfied that they received fair value for what was incurred. It is easy to have short-term "feel good" experiences at a chiropractor's or physical therapist's office. However, patients these days are more value-conscious and will demand to see overall progress in their condition as opposed to merely temporary relief where the pain only comes back in equal intensity. If the patient believes that relief was only temporary and the symptoms returned in only a few days, they will quickly discharge themselves from care.

Causation

Another critically important area in documentation of injuries in the personal injury or forensic setting is the issue of causation. In Utah, causation is largely determined by symptomology. I have spoken with many physicians, particularly MD's, who believe that they only need to treat conditions or symptoms and need not be worried about causation.

That may be true for ordinary patients, but when a traumatic event is involved, the number one question that the court will ask is, "What caused this injury?" The human body is a marvelous creation, but it is subject to a number of potential injuries which can cause painful and sometime lifelong symptoms. The interplay between bone, cartilage, disc, ligaments, muscles, and nerves is complex and fragile. If you as a physician need to take courses in basic biomechanical issues in order to gain an understanding of the dynamics of motor vehicle accidents, slip-and-fall injuries, or other kinds of forensic events, then do so. Orthopedic, neurologic and muscular-ligamentous injuries ordinarily do not just "happen." They are generally caused, brought about, or aggravated by something.

In every forensic setting, it is important for the physician to include a statement as to the origin of the patient's problems. In order to do so, it is not necessary that the physician be 100% certain. The physician only has to be convinced by a "preponderance of the evidence." This means that the physician only has to believe that it is "probable" or "more likely than not" that the subject traumatic event (motor vehicle accident, fall, etc.) caused, precipitated, or aggravated the patient's symptoms. Put another way, if the physician is only 51% sure or convinced that the traumatic event brought about the patient's condition, that is sufficient under the law to say that the patient's conditions were brought about or "caused by" the subject compensatory event. This decision only has to be based upon a reasonable degree of probability or certainty within that physician's line of specialty. In short, "Doctor, what is the most likely explanation for this patient's injuries?"

This level of probability or reasonable certainty often cuts against the grain of most medical school decision making or causation algorithms. In medical school, a physician is taught to rule out causes in a truth-functional logical pattern of thinking. This pattern has the good physician, one by one, ruling out the entire world of possibilities. That may be an extremely effective method for the brilliant Dr. House. However, in the civil courtroom there is simply not time to demand such a high level of certainty or we would never be able to reach any decision or conclusion. The "preponderance of the evidence" burden of proof is applicable only to civil courtrooms. In criminal courtrooms often a different standard of proof called "beyond a reasonable doubt" of evidence may be used. However, that level of certainty is neither necessary nor demanded in a civil setting where the claims in a personal injury lawsuit will be brought.

I recommend to each physician, who has a patient indicate that his or her injuries stemmed from any kind of traumatic event, include in his notes or records a statement relative to causation. This causation statement will have the effect of minimizing the demand or request for either narrative reports or a need for the physicians to have to testify in depositions or trial. Many physicians erroneously believe that not discussing the issue of causation will guarantee they will not be involved in legal actions. That is not true. If the records do not say it, the attorneys will have to request a report or deposition in order to ask the physician directly. Even if the physician believes that there is no causal link between the event and the alleged injuries, the defense attorney may be interested in subpoenaing the physician to trial to give that testimony as proof that some or all of the plaintiff's claims are unfounded. Likewise, the statement of causation is also important in allowing for the subrogation or reimbursement of health insurance carriers' payments. Voice your opinion in your notes and you will have to do so less often in court.

A causation conclusion is easier to reach than many physicians might think. If the patient had no symptoms before an event and the symptoms began immediately or within a short time thereafter the event, and if the symptoms are the kind one would reasonably expect to have been produced by such an event, it is a pretty good indication that, at a minimum, the subject event is highly suspect for being the cause of the symptoms. The suspicion that the event caused the symptoms is substantially raised further when there is no other reasonable and probable explanation that can be given for the relatively sudden onset of symptoms. Under most circumstances, the above set of facts would lead a normally competent physician to reasonably conclude, within a reasonable degree of medical or chiropractic probability, that it is more likely than not that the subject event "caused" or "aggravated" the symptoms producing the injuries.

The most common challenge medical practitioners find on the issue of causation is when a patient's symptoms are multi-factorial in nature. This is usually the case when a patient has a number of naturally caused degenerative processes in the body that make a patient more predisposed to a certain condition than would be an otherwise healthy individual. In this situation, the physician must make his best non-arbitrary judgment call, based on as much reliable evidence as possible to apportion the probable causes of the patient's symptoms. It is not an exact science, and, it is ultimately left to the jury to make a decision as guided by the evidence.

Many physical conditions are non-symptomatic or latent. These conditions may lie dormant for many years before being activated or brought to life by a traumatic event. The dormancy of a condition is not held against the victim in his or her efforts to claim it as being a result of the accident or traumatic event. Put another way, the persons causing the accident take the victim as they find them. If the victim is a healthy athlete who is hardly injured from the wrongdoing, then the tort feasor or perpetrator of the act lucks out and will likely be held to a smaller verdict against them. Conversely, if the perpetrator injures a frail, elderly person, the verdict may be greater. That is the risk the wrongdoer takes in causing the wrong.

Objective Proof

Closely related to the issue of causation is the use of examination components for measurement and objectification of the injuries. A common defense question in a deposition that I hear goes something like this: "Doctor, isn't it true that the only thing that you really have to go on here is the patient's subjective complaints of pain?" If I am at that deposition, I hope I never hear my client's physician say "yes" to that question. Even with simple muscle spasms, a physician's trained fingers running down the spine can sense heat changes and sometimes the actual movement of muscle twitching in spasm. It is generally not possible for a patient to fake or artificially create his or her own muscle spasms. Can another trained physician likewise come and feel the same muscle spasms including temperature differences and vibrations? Of course! Therefore, even simple spinal palpation is an objective measurement of paraspinal muscle spasms. How many vertebral levels were involved in the spasm? Did that number of levels decrease in subsequent re-examinations? If so, objective progress was made between the two examinations. Appropriate use of radiology, including radiologic measurements in millimeters of translation, Penning angles, and other measurements can be used to objectify the extent and degree of problems. In your report, examination notes, or narrative do not simply say, "subluxation" or "loss of curve." While these statements may be true and correct, they are not as helpful as a statement that actually indicates measurement.

Numbers of orthopedic and neurologic tests which are found to be positive can also be utilized as a means to measure objective progress.

Orthopedic and neurologic tests are tests used across the board by MD's, DO's, and DC's in evaluation of the kinds of red flags which such tests tend to reveal. The manner in which these tests are performed varies very little between the disciplines, and generally another physician of the same or different discipline can reproduce the tests and come up with the same conclusions. Therefore, these tests are objective in nature. Did the amount of orthopedic or neurologic tests which were found to be positive decrease in the subsequent re-examination? If so, then progress has been made.

Another critically important area to measure status and progress is the range of motion measurements. It is not nearly enough to anymore to say, "range of motion decreased." It is far more helpful to give the normal or expected range of motion in degrees and the measured range of motion in degrees found in the particular patient. Therefore, if painful muscle spasms are restricting movement, the reader of the report, be it an adjuster, an attorney, or a juror can see exactly what you are talking about. Likewise, subsequent measurements on re-examinations can tell exactly how much improvement has been made.

"Malingering" or "Non-Organic" Findings

A final area that needs to be added to the list of important component of personal injury or forensic medicine of chiropractic care is the subject of "malingering" or "non-organic" findings. Every adjuster is suspicious for it and looks for it. Likewise, every perspective juror believes that the plaintiff is probably faking his or her injuries at least to some degree. Although Wadell's signs were never intended to be a litmus test for malingering, being familiar with Wadell's signs can be helpful. There are numerous other malingering tests which most physicians are familiar with from distraction to simple repeated tests. The physician should include in his notes that he is concerned about the potential for malingering or non-organic findings in a compensatory situation, and in fact has tested the plaintiff and found that the plaintiff was not malingering and gave consistent, true and faithful effort and responses. If that is not the case, every good plaintiff's attorney wants to be the first to know if his client is either faking it or trying to stretch the truth. The attorney representing a patient needs to know if the patient has the potential for histrionics as a witness. In contrast to images presented by the media, hyper drama does not play well in the courtroom. Juries simply do not buy it and often respond negatively to those witnesses or claimants who attempt it.

In my experience as an attorney, I find that the issue of secondary gain motivation is far exaggerated by the defense industry. I have never had someone (even in big cases where the payout has been large) tell me they were grateful for the money and wanted to attempt the injury again. As a general rule, the paltry compensation that the people receive through the court system is never equivalent to the amount of blood and pain the patient has gone through.

Conclusion

Personal injury or forensic healthcare may seem to some physicians like it is more work than it is worth. However, the things I have suggested above are nothing more than good medicine and good chiropractic care. An increasing number of physicians of all different types of training are realizing that the compensation for personal injury treatment that is properly documented, as outlined above, is more fair and complete than the ridiculous reimbursement schedules demanded by all other types of health insurance and government health care reimbursement programs such as Medicare and Medicaid. However, that rate of reimbursement in the forensic setting is only provided when the care is demonstrated to be justified and appropriate.

The current system of justice that we have is under constant attack by forces with political agendas that would take away the rights of victims to be fully and completely compensated for what they have lost. Tort reform proposals not only attack victims but also inherently attack the physicians who care for victims. Few physicians limit their practice exclusively to people that have been injured in traumatic events caused by third parties. Nevertheless, most physicians realize that treatment of personal injury victims is and can be a very valuable component to their overall practice of medicine or chiropractic care. If handled correctly, trauma patients will come back for other care and refer their family and friends.

If any physician reading this has any specific questions or interest in the subject matter, I welcome the inquiry. You may contact me at bryanlarson@larsonlawutah.com or visit www.larsonlawutah.com for other contact information.

> Thank you so much for your help after that awful car accident. Thank you for dealing with the various insurance companies, especially PEHP and Medicare. It was so nice to be able to call a skilled attorney when we had a question and it would be answered. We so appreciated your kindness and help when we needed it.
>
> ~Archie & Sylvia

Treatment Protocols

A cervical collar should not be used for longer than 72 hours as it may lead to prolonged inactivity.[89] *[Author—"Motion is life" in the human body. Regional immobilization results in muscles atrophy, joints degeneration and further tissue necrosis. The outcome is a greater need for rehabilitation therapy. This can lead to increase in cost and a decrease in patient recovery. In some cases chronic/permanent dysfunction or disability may be the end result.]*

Helping the patient return to normal activities of daily living should be encouraged as soon as possible to maximize and expedite full recovery.[90] *[Author—It is sound advice to work to get patients back to their normal "Activities of Daily Living" as soon as possible. Depending on the severity of the injury the doctor should be advising the patient to refrain from certain exercises and activities **for a time** but monitor and advise when they can be released to slowly reinstate their normal activities.]*

If there is no improvement or minimal improvement in 6 to 12 weeks then interdisciplinary or team care is warranted. *[Author – Brilliant! Whiplash Associated Disorders are complicated and often require "specialists" and interdisciplinary care.]*

Responsible first contact physicians (ER doctors, general practitioners, and pediatricians) who see or treat patients with whiplash associated disorder should build a contact list of other physicians specializing in this area. If the "first contact physicians" simply offers a prescription

---

89. Gurumoorthy D, Twomey L (1996). "The Quebec Task Force on Whiplash-Associated Disorders". Spine 21 (7): 897-8.

90. Gurumoorthy D, Twomey L (1996). "The Quebec Task Force on Whiplash-Associated Disorders". Spine 21 (7): 897-8.

of care similar to what is suggested by the National Institute for Neurological Disorders, then the likelihood of a negative long-term outcome is exponentially increased.

This being said, life threatening, serious injuries, or suspected serious injuries should be properly evaluated, diagnosed and treated at an emergency facility.

Less serious injuries should be evaluated at an urgent care facility or by a chiropractic physician certified in motor vehicle occupant injury.

According to research, the road to MMI is reached faster, with less expense and fewer chronic symptoms when chiropractic, massage and physical therapy are introduced early in the tissue recovery stages. None of these three physical medicines are a replacement for the other. They synergistically help advance tissues recovery with less residual scar tissue. This gives the healing tissue a greater number of natural parallel fibers vs. unwanted scar tissue.

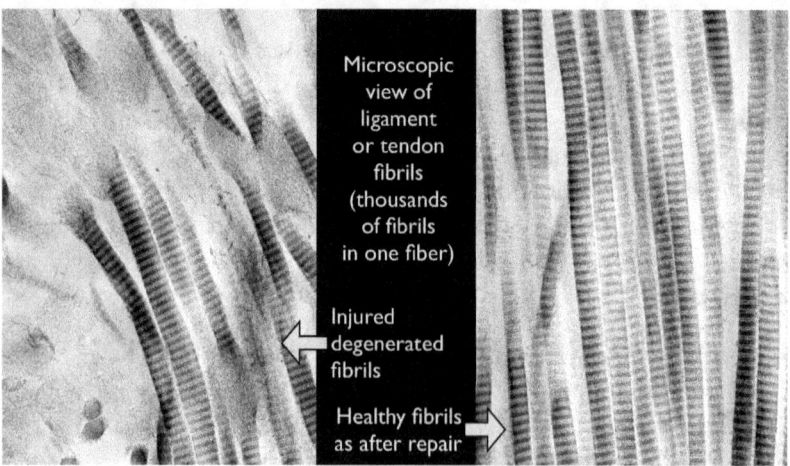

Microscopic view of ligament or tendon fibrils (thousands of fibrils in one fiber)

Injured degenerated fibrils

Healthy fibrils as after repair

Even with serious or life threatening injuries, once the dangers are averted, it is important that physicians do not simply treat symptoms with pain medication and muscle relaxers but rather, to rehabilitate the injured soft tissues with chiropractic, massage and physical therapy.

The following flow chart illustrates very simply how a patient should flow through the current health care and recovery system. It shows how any soft tissue injury should be graded by a certified specialist physician, grading I through V. It also shows how the health care team of physicians can best work together if symptoms are not improving with soft tissue rehabilitative care.

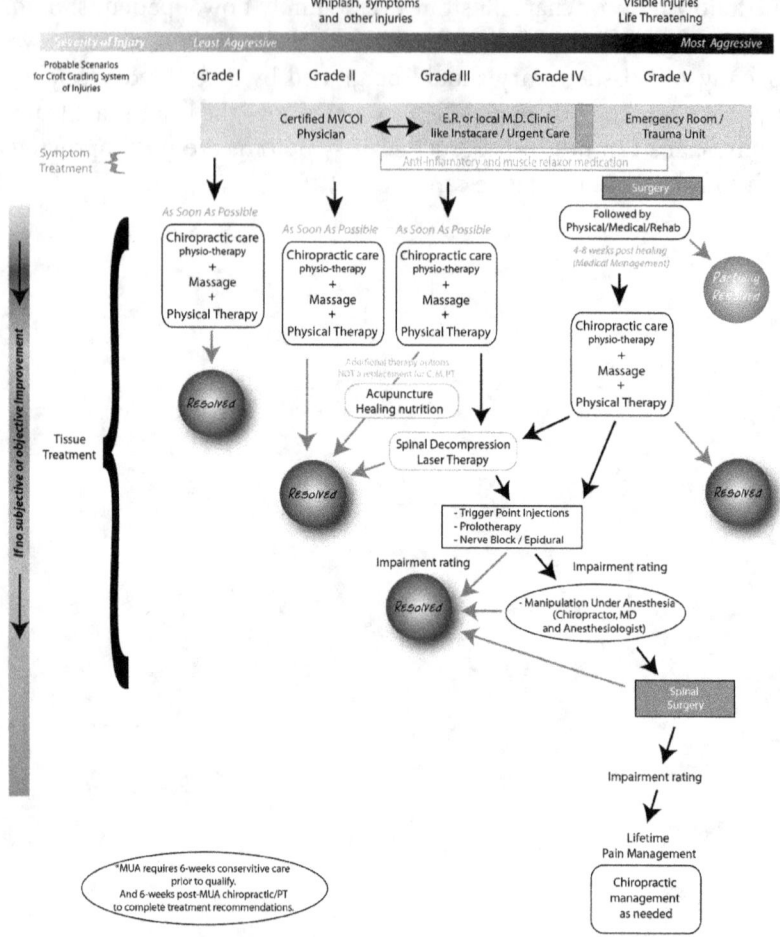

A full-size color version of the flow chart is available at:

http://www.drjayshetlin.com/resources/

NOTES

Epilogue

Unfortunately, cervical soft tissue injuries and cervical acceleration deceleration (CAD) injuries are often overlooked and under diagnosed. This results in untreated or undertreated injuries. This problem begins with a population that is poorly educated in the importance of early intervention. This intervention is essential regardless of present symptoms.

The lack of information available to the public is complicated by emergency care physicians, general practitioners and pediatricians who are not trained in the detection of these conditions and are unwilling to refer patients to CAD injury specialists. The problem is ultimately exacerbated by the number of insurance companies who minimize or discredit the existence of these injuries so that they can fight to deny proper care.

Research shows that human soft tissues have a tensile resist threshold. Shear force, as in auto accidents, with a change of velocity as little as 2.5 miles per hour can result in micro tears to human soft tissue. A crash resulting in a change of velocity of only a few miles per hour or more, when applied to human ligament and muscle tissue, can result in soft tissue injuries (especially in the cervical spine).

Some insurance companies may try to downplay the seriousness of these injuries. They may even question the existence of soft tissue injuries—but they are real. The research is clear. These injuries take place every day in motor vehicle collisions, even in low-energy collisions. In some states the word "whiplash" is looked at as a negative label because they see patients with whiplash as opportunists just seeking financial gain or narcotic medication for recreation, thus downplaying the seriousness of CAD injuries.

Whiplash and soft tissue injuries are serious and need to be treated properly with a team approach by physicians and caregivers who have the best interests of their patients at heart. The right medical and chiropractic care at the right time will save billions of dollars in wasted insurance money and litigation costs. Trying to fix the unfixable late-onset chronic problems related to MVCs is expensive and often far less successful.

The auto makers have made great strides in the improvement and safety of automobiles. How and when a motor vehicle accident will happen is completely unpredictable. The exact dynamics, occupant position, and the full extent of the physical forces any given driver or passenger will experience in a motor vehicle incident is impossible to predict. Thoughtful engineering is applied, vehicles are sold and fingers are crossed as we hope to see fewer serious or deadly injuries from car crashes. Try as we might to prevent them, while the population of drivers on the road continues to grow, collisions continue to happen. The result is a staggering amount of injuries each day.

Research shows that chiropractic care from a certified specialist [91] is the most effective treatment for CAD disorders. When properly combined with physical therapy, massage and modern medical techniques, the positive results are even greater. In difficult cases where there is a plateau in recovery or the desired MMI is not reached, manipulation under anesthesia is often the preferred 'pre-surgery' option yielding a staggering success rate when performed as an interdisciplinary team effort.

It is my hope that physical medicine (chiropractic, physical therapy and massage) can work in kind with general medicine (ER doctors, general practitioners, pediatricians, etc) to more fully treat and rehabilitate victims of motor vehicle collisions so that each patient can achieve a true, ethical and effective maximum medical improvement.

---

91. Many doctors of chiropractic advertise "auto accident specialist" after taking a weekend seminar or with absolutely no additional training. Their care is definitely better than no chiropractic care but the difference in utilizing a CERTIFIED specialist is exponentially better. Chiropractic physicians who want to specialize in auto injury rehabilitation need to certify. To dabble in the auto accident market without the proper training hurts the patient and patient's legal case far more than one might realize. This comment is not intended to offend but is spoken from experience. Those who are untrained can be unaware of what they don't know and patients can suffer because of it. More information is available at www.personalinjurytraininginstitute.org.

Done properly, physicians can substantially reduce the number of patients suffering from long-term or chronic pain resulting from motor vehicle collision injuries.

The answers to affordable health and healing, less insurance expense and more joyful patients lie with us, as physicians, keeping to the Hippocratic oath we swore to uphold.

> *"I will not be ashamed to say 'I know not,' nor will I fail to call in my colleagues when the skills of another are needed for a patient's recovery."*

Research

The following is a small portion of the research available on the topics addressed in this book.

- Abridgements are compliments of Dr. Dan Murphy.
- Key points [**KP**] from the author are formatted as **bold text**.

The Cervical Syndrome as a Cause of Migraine —Journal of the American Medical Women's Association December 1947, Vol. 2, No. 12, pp. 529–534
Ruth Jackson, MD

"Dr. Ruth Jackson was the first woman physician to be elected to membership in the American Academy of Orthopedic Surgery and to be certified by the American Board of Orthopedic Surgery."

This Author Notes:

At least half of patients suffering from cervical syndrome causing shoulder disability will also complain of headache as one of their principle symptoms. The cervical syndrome is caused by "cervical nerve root irritation." There is a relationship between the cervical syndrome, cervical nerve root irritation, and the autonomic nervous system.

[KP] **"The cervical nerve roots are more vulnerable to pressure or irritation from ruptured discs, hemorrhage, inflammatory processes of the capsules, spurs, and abnormal motion of the joints due to relaxation or tearing of the capsular and ligamentous structures."** [NOTE: "abnormal motion of the joints"]

Sympathetic nerves that originate at the T1 and T2 levels ascend into the cervical spine becoming the cervical sympathetic trunk, with its inferior, middle, and superior ganglia.

"From the superior cervical ganglia, grey rami communicante postganglionic sympathetic efferents pass from the ganglia to the anterior rami of the upper four cervical nerves."

"Other postganglionic [sympathetic] fibers travel via the internal carotid and ophthalmic arteries to join the orbit and supply the dilator muscle of the pupil and smooth muscles of the upper eyelid, the back of the orbit, and the blood vessels of the eyeball."

"Irritation of the cervical nerve roots before they divide into anterior and posterior primary rami may occur as a result of any mechanical derangement in or about the intervertebral foramina. The most common cause of irritation is abnormal motion or subluxation of the joints due to relaxation of the capsular and ligamentous structures following trauma."

Following whiplash trauma, as time passes, "abnormal motion or subluxations of the articular processes, will cause irritation of one or more nerve roots."

[KP] **"Rupture of one or two intervertebral discs may occur then or later as a result of a trivial injury such as a sudden motion of the neck."**

[KP] **"Any unguarded motion or prolonged relaxation of the neck in one position may allow a subluxation to occur," which may cause cervical nerve root irritation.**

In a patient with a "crick in the neck" the "crick is a result of cervical nerve root irritation from subluxation, pressure from a ruptured disc, or irritation from an inflammatory process in the capsules."

In reviewing the history of 200 patients with neck symptoms, "the accidents had occurred from a few hours to thirty years before the patients were seen in our clinic, and symptoms had been present from the time of the accident to many years after the injury."

64% of the patients with neck symptoms were women, and age ranged from 7 to 70 years.

[KP] If the C1-C2-C3 nerve roots are involved, typical symptoms include:

- Neck pain
- Limitation of neck motion
- Headache, which usually "starts at the back of the neck or base of the skull and then involves one or both sides of the head, and pain in the mastoid region or in the ears"
- Blurring of the vision (found in 20% of patients)
- Dizziness and nausea
- Numbness of the sides of the neck
- Tightness of the neck muscles
- Pain in the supraclavicular region

"If C4 is involved there may be shortness of breath, palpitations, anterior chest pain and pain and muscle spasm in the muscles supplied by C4."

"When the lower nerve roots are involved, the symptoms are commensurate with the segmental character of the nerve roots which are irritated." These patients often have numbness or tingling of the fingers when they awaken.

[KP] "In all instances the symptoms are brought on or aggravated by certain motions of the neck or by maintaining certain positions over long periods of time," including:

- Sewing
- Reading
- Writing
- Cooking
- Driving
- Poor sleeping postures

[KP] "There is always tenderness to deep pressure over the vertebrae, usually just lateral to the spinous process of the side of the nerve root irritation."

"If the irritation is above the fourth nerve root, there may be tender areas over the occiput and the mastoid. If the fourth nerve root is involved, there may be tender areas in the ridge of the trapezius and/or in the sterno-mastoid muscles."

5% of patients will have a dilation of the pupil on the side of nerve root irritation.

"The most constant finding in all of our cases was the presence of myalgic areas in the upper or lower cervical portion of the rhomboid muscles which is indicative of fifth nerve root irritation."

"Often there seems to be localized fibrosis of the muscle. Irritation causes spasm which if allowed to persist causes ischemia with eventual formation of localized fibrosis." *Important, Fibrosis of Repair

Irritation of the fourth nerve root may cause referred pain to the diaphragm, the pericardium, and shoulder.

"X-rays of the cervical spine are of real diagnostic aid in cervical nerve root irritation." Dr. Jackson recommends a Davis [92] series of X-rays be taken in all cervical trauma cases, and emphasizes the importance of maximum flexion and maximum extension views.

"In 70% of our cases there was obliteration of the curve and in 20% of there was a segmental reversal of the [cervical lordotic] curve."

Dr. Jackson calls abnormal forward or backward slipping of a vertebral segment on flexion or extension a subluxation, stating "90% of our patients had forward subluxations and 56% had backward subluxations."

96% of patients with cervical syndrome headaches will show subluxations at more than one level, and in 77% the subluxation was of C2 on C3, irritating the C3 nerve root. "This indicates that the irritation of the third cervical nerve root must have been responsible for the greatest percentage of headache."

Dr. Jackson believes that the blurring of the vision (and ipsilateral pupil dilation, when present) seen in many cervical syndrome/headache patients is caused by irritation of the superior sympathetic ganglion caused by cervical muscle spasm.

---

92. Davis series radiographs are specific to chiropractic. There are several series including 5-views, 7-views, and 9-views.

She maintains that "cervical nerve root irritation (C3 usually) is an etiological factor in migraine."

She recommends the use of a cervical contour pillow for rest and healing. She states "the contour pillow fits the natural curve of the neck. We then made X-ray films to prove that the contour pillow maintains the neck in a straight position while the conventional pillow causes slight flexion of the neck." "This pillow has been our greatest adjunct in the treatment of cervical nerve root irritation."

Conclusion

"The upper cervical nerve roots supply the major portion of the scalp, the middle and posterior scalene, and the sternomastoid muscles. Spasm of these muscles which surround the superior sympathetic ganglia may, and do, cause irritation of the ganglia or the postganglionic fibers. Therefore, irritation of the upper cervical nerve roots (C2 toC4) with or without the associated irritation of the cervical sympathetics can certainly cause symptoms of migraine."

**Putting the 5 mph injury threshold to the test Brian Henderson reveals the results of his extensive research into the impact of low-speed-change collisions Personal Injury Law Journal
September 2006**

Brian Henderson, Managing Director of GBB Ltd Forensic Collision Investigation and Research

This Author Notes:

It is often claimed that below a certain speed change "injury will not occur," and this threshold is purported to be 5 mph.

[KP] Collisions between motor vehicles and the occupants of those vehicles must conform to Newton's Laws of Motion.

"Historically, the argument about injury or likelihood of injury had been the domain of the medical experts, albeit without any true scientific evidence on which to base an opinion."

[KP] A struck vehicle will accelerate forward, with or without vehicle damage. This will cause accelerations of the occupant's chest and head.

This author and his colleagues have produced crashes resulting in a change in velocity of 5.97 mph of the struck vehicle. This caused a 4.7 g acceleration of the occupant's chest and an 8.3 g acceleration of the occupant's head. The difference between the head and chest acceleration was 3.6 g. This resulted in the symptoms of strains and headaches.

[KP] However, this research also showed that not all occupants reacted in the same manner to the same change in velocity.

This author and his colleagues have also produced collisions that produced a change in velocity between 2.8 to 3.1 mph. This resulted in a chest acceleration of 2.93 g and a head acceleration of 3.46 g. the difference between the chest and head acceleration was 0.53 g.

[KP] This author states:

- "It is my opinion that beyond a speed change of 5 mph, the risk of injury is high."
- "The risk [of injury] between 3 mph and 5 mph [speed change] is a grey area that would need further exploration, and injury cannot be ruled out."
- "The risk [of injury] below 3 mph [speed change] is minimal."

Low Impact Collisions and Injury
Rene Cailliet, MD, 2006

"Simulated impacts have been studied extensively and essentially confirm that a low-speed impact with minimal or no damage to the impacted vehicle can and does cause significant musculoskeletal injury to the driver's or occupant's head and neck." p. 4

"It has been shown that high speeds are not specifically pertinent in determining the extent of the [whiplash] injuries sustained." p. 32

"Numerous injuries result from vehicular accidents even when the impacts are not very big and there is minimal damage to both vehicles." p. 87

"In many instances, a person experiences whiplash after a vehicle accident that has caused little significant damage to either vehicle." p. 100

Whiplash-Associated Diseases
Rene Cailliet, MD

Professor Emeritus at the University of Southern California School of Medicine and a clinical professor at the Department of Physical Medicine Rehabilitation at the UCLA School of Medicine. Dr. Cailliet has written 17 texts on musculoskeletal problems that have sold more than 1.2 million copies.

American Medical Association 2006—Acceleration of Degenerative Disc Disease Following Whiplash Injuries

"Follow-up roentgenograms taken an average of 7 years after injury in one series of patients without prior roentgenographic evidence of disc disease indicated that 39% had developed degenerative disc disease at one or more disc levels since injury."

[KP] The above paragraph correlates perfectly with the author's findings on page 41.

There was an expected incidence of 6% degenerative change in the population over this period of time. "Thus, it appeared that the injury had started the slow process of disc degeneration."

"In another follow-up study of patients with similar injuries but with preexisting degenerative changes in the neck, it was observed that after an average of 7 years 39% had residual symptoms, and roentgenographic evidence of new degenerative change at another level occurred in 55%."

"Of considerable interest was the finding in both series that there was no statistical correlation between the development of degenerative changes and continued symptoms."

[KP]This is significant in the common misunderstanding that arthritis or disc/joint degenerative disease is "just part of getting old." *It clearly is not.* **It is trauma or dysfunction in a joint that, over time, will lead to the degenerative changes. These changes may not directly cause pain**

or symptoms for years; however, rehabilitation of late onset symptoms is much more difficult when degenerative arthritis is present. This is yet another reason why early intervention and proper rehabilitation are so important to prevent long-term, late onset or chronic symptoms.

Kinematic Cervical Spine Magnetic Resonance Imaging in Low-Impact Trauma Assessment

Seminars in Ultrasound, CT, and MRI
June 2009; Volume 30; Number 3; pp. 168–173

Vincenzo Giuliano, MD, Antonio Pinto, MD, PhD, and Mariano Scaglione, MD

Dr. Giuliano is from Nova Southeastern University, College of Medicine, Winter Springs, Florida.

From Abstract:

Kinematic magnetic resonance imaging can be implemented as a noninvasive adjunct examination for injuries in the cervical spine in the clinical assessment of ligamentous, disc, and soft-tissue injuries, as a basis for determining medical vs. surgical management, and in establishing the degree of functional clinical impairment.

These Authors Also Note:

"The cervical spine is particularly susceptible to acceleration and deceleration injuries resulting from impact trauma."

"Low-impact collisions result in acceleration and deceleration of the head and neck, also known as whiplash."

In the biomechanics of whiplash the cervical spine forms an S-shaped curve, with hyperflexion in the upper cervical spinal segments and simultaneous hyperextension in the lower cervical spinal segments.

"Approximately 60% of whiplash injuries are occult to magnetic resonance imaging (MRI) and include occult soft-tissue, intervertebral disc, and ligamentous injuries, accounting for approximately 90% of injuries missed by MRI."

"Cervical instability is defined as angular motion greater than 11 degrees, or translation of greater than 3 mm, for contiguous spinal segments."

"The optimal period for performing evaluation of the cervical spine using kinematic MRI methods is 12 weeks post-injury, following resolution of muscle spasm."

"Initial radiographic series should include the anteroposterior and lateral flexion/extension views. The most common finding is straightening of the cervical spine, with either loss or reversal of the normal lordotic curve."

"MRI is clinically indicated in the setting of persistent arm pain, neurologic deficits, and clinical signs of nerve root compression."

"MRI offers the best noninvasive and detailed evaluation of the intervertebral discs, soft-tissue structures, and spinal cord but is considered unreliable in the detection of subtle annular disc tears."

"Hyperflexion injuries can evade radiologic detection."

"Kinematic MRI provides the most optimal means of detecting subtle hyperflexion injuries and annular disc tears, in addition to evaluating segmental spinal motion and cervical lordosis patterns."

"Kinematic MRI, in contradistinction to other imaging methods, such as lateral lexion/extension radiographs and videofluoroscopy, provides accurate assessment of spinal canal stenosis."

"Clinical criteria for kinematic MRI evaluations include the persistence of signs and symptoms during the subacute period, including localized neck pain and radiculopathy, despite clinically resolved muscle spasm.

"The kinematic MRI evaluation is typically coordinated with manipulative therapy and rehabilitation programs.

The kinematic MRI protocol should be performed as an additional sequencefollowing the static cervical MRI examination. "The sagittal T2 fast-spin-echo (FSE) scan sequence is the most optimal imaging parameter and provides the most accurate and reliable diagnostic information in distinguishing soft-tissue contrast between aqueous structures, such as nucleus pulposus and cerebral spinal fluid, from ligamentous structures."

Typical normal, non-injured findings with kinematic cervical spine MRI:

- A stepwise segmental motion starting at C1-C2 and extending to the lower cervical spinal segments in a coordinated and orderly pattern.
- A lordotic cervical curve.
- "Hypolordosis with normal segmental motion is generally observed in 4%-7% of cases, representing a normal variant."
- A fanlike and unrestricted motion of the spinous processes is.
- Between 45-60 degrees of cervical spine flexion.
- Between 50-70 degrees of cervical spin extension.
- Small asymptomatic bulging discs in 2% of patients.

Kinematic cervical spine MRI evaluations in injured subjects usually reveal:

- Injury to the joint capsule, interspinous/supraspinous ligaments, and ventral annulus fibrosus.
- The posterior longitudinal ligament is intact.
- "Hypolordosis is invariably present, with notable segmental motion restriction characterized by an absence of the normal fanlike movements of the spinous processes of C4 through C7."
- "Flexion appears disproportionally restricted compared to extension, with exacerbation of symptoms, including headache, arm pain, and arm numbness."

"Maximum medical improvement of all whiplash injuries is generally achieved within 2 years."

Conclusions

"Kinematic MRI evaluations of the cervical spine can provide a valuable adjunct method to the standard static cervical spine MR examination." "Kinematic MRI is clinically indicated in patients with whiplash injuries with one or more persistent neurologic deficits or clinical signs and symptoms beyond the normal and expected recovery period, generally within 8-12 weeks."

Prognostic factors of whiplash-associated disorders:
A systematic review of prospective cohort studies Pain
July 2003, Vol. 104, pp. 303-322

Gwendolijne G.M. Scholten-Peeters, Arianne P. Verhagen, Geertruida E. Bekkering, Danielle A.W.M. van der Windt, Les Barnsley, Rob A.B. Ostendorp, Erik J.M. Hendriks

From Abstract

We present a systematic review of prospective cohort studies. Our aim was to assess prognostic factors associated with functional recovery of patients with whiplash injuries.

The failure of some patients to recover following whiplash injury has been linked to a number of prognostic factors. However, there is some inconsistency in the literature and there have been no systematic attempts to analyze the level of evidence for prognostic factors in whiplash recovery.

Studies were selected for inclusion following a comprehensive search of MEDLINE, EMBASE, CINAHL, the database of the Dutch Institute of Allied Health Professions up until April 2002 and hand searches of the reference lists of retrieved articles. Studies were selected if the objective was to assess prognostic factors associated with recovery; the design was a prospective cohort study; the study population included at least an identifiable subgroup of patients suffering from a whiplash injury; and the paper was a full report published in English, German, French or Dutch. The methodological quality was independently assessed by two reviewers. A study was considered to be of 'high quality' if it satisfied at least 50% of the maximum available quality score. Two independent reviewers extracted data and the association between prognostic factors and functional recovery was calculated in terms of risk estimates.

Fifty papers reporting on twenty-nine cohorts were included in the review. Twelve cohorts were considered to be of 'high quality'. Because of the heterogeneity of patient selection, type of prognostic factors and outcome measures, no statistical pooling was able to be performed.

Strong evidence was found for high initial pain intensity being an adverse prognostic factor.

There was strong evidence that for older age, female gender, high acute psychological responses, angular deformity of the neck, rear-end collision, and compensation not being associated with an adverse prognosis. **In other words, were all complicating factors overlooked in the prognosis that made for a less than favorable outcome.**

Several physical (e.g. restricted range of motion, high number of complaints), psychosocial (previous psychological problems), neuropsychosocial factors (nervousness), crash related (e.g. accident on highway) and treatment related factors (need to resume physiotherapy) showed limited prognostic value for functional recovery.

High initial pain intensity is an important predictor for delayed functional recovery for patients with whiplash injury.

Often mentioned factors like age, gender and compensation do not seem to be of prognostic value.

Scientific information about prognostic factors can guide physicians or other care providers to direct treatment and to probably prevent chronicity.

These Authors Also Note:

[KP] **"The term whiplash is defined as an acceleration-deceleration mechanism of energy transfer to the neck that results from rear-end or side-impact MVCs, but can also result from diving or other mishaps."**

"The impact results in bony or soft-tissue injuries (whiplash injury), which in turn may lead to a variety of clinical manifestations called whiplash-associated disorders (WAD)."

[KP] **"A significant proportion [of whiplash injured patients] develop chronic and often intractable and disabling symptoms."**

[KP] Studies on whiplash-injured patients report:

- 19–60% still have complaints at six months after a whiplash injury
- 13–50% are still absent from work or not able to perform their usual activities at 6 months

[These studies refer to individuals who did not seek or were not referred to physicians specializing in the treatment of whiplash injuries]

It is problematic to assess factors for delayed recovery utilizing diverse definitions of recovery such as pain, duration of absence from usual activities, or time-to-claim-closure.

[KP] **The 1995 Quebec Task Force (QTF) on WAD did not provide evidence-based recommendations concerning prognostic factors for recovery because there was a shortage of adequate prognostic studies.**

Whiplash Injury

Journal of Bone and Joint Surgery (British)

July 2009, Vol. 91B, no. 7, pp. 845–850
G. Bannister, R. Amirfeyz, S. Kelley, M. Gargan

Comments From Dan Murphy

This is a review article that has 100 references. Two of the authors, Gordon Bannister and Martin Gargan are probably the most published individuals in history on long-term recovery outcomes of whiplash injuries.

From Abstract

Most whiplash injury cases occur as the result of rear-end vehicle collisions at speeds of less than 14 miles per hour.

Patients present with neck pain and stiffness, occipital headache, thoracolumbar back pain and upper-limb pain and paraesthesia.

Over 66% make a full recovery and 2% are permanently disabled.

The outcome can be predicted in 70% after three months.

These Authors Make The Following Key Points:

- Patients who sustain low-velocity whiplash injuries often will have more pain than those who sustain a fracture.

- Patients who sustain low-velocity whiplash injuries often will have more psychological distress than those who sustain a fracture.

- Although the term "whiplash" is often credited to HD Crowe's presentation of 8 injured cases as a result of rear-end vehicle collisions to the Western Orthopedic Association in 1928, the injury was recognized at least as early as 1882 when it was referred to as "spinal concussion" or "railway spine."
- 90% of all road-traffic collisions occur at speeds less than 14 mph and "it is in these that whiplash occurs."
- "Since the mid-1950s, it has been recognized that the disability from whiplash is associated less with tire skid marks or the degree of vehicle damage than the effect of differential velocity on the head and upper torso."
- **[KP] Rear-end collisions are associated with more severe symptoms than collisions from any other direction.**
- **[KP] Being rear-ended by a larger/heavier vehicle increases inertial injuries.**
- **[KP] Because women have a thinner, less rigid neck they have twice the whiplash injury rate as men.**
- **[KP] Head restraints that are too low act as a fulcrum and increase neck injury greater than no head restraint at all.**
- The best head restraints are high and positioned to reduce the posterior excursion of the head.
- It has been known since human volunteer rear-end crash testing in 1956 that whiplash trauma produced a "cracking sound somewhere in the vicinity of the cervical spine and [the volunteer] suffered pain for some time afterwards."
- All human volunteer rear-end crash tests at collision speeds of 5 mph have produced neck pain in a proportion of their subjects.
- A change of velocity of 2.5 mph was sufficient to cause symptoms and a speed of 8.7 mph was needed to cause damage to a vehicle. **[The reference for this statement is a colleague, Charles Davis, DC, in a 1998 article he published in the Journal of Manipulative and Physiological Therapeutics]**
- Only 15% of those involved in a rear-end collision will experience pain and go to the doctor.
- **[KP] Of those attending an Emergency Department:**
  - 37% experienced immediate pain

- 62–65% experienced pain within 12 hours
- 90% experienced pain within 24 hours
- 10% experienced pain after 24 hours
- 50% of all cases of upper-limb pain and weakness occur more than a week after the injury.
- [KP] 66% of women experience sufficient pain to take time off work for 2–69 days after the accident.
- [KP] The most common whiplash-injury symptoms are:
  - **Neck pain**
  - **Neck stiffness**
  - **Occipital headache**
  - **Thoracolumbar back pain**
  - **Upper limb paraesthesia**
- 5–9% of whiplash-injured patients develop subacromial impingement syndrome.
- 38% of whiplash-injured patients will suffer irritation of the brachial plexus.
- Symptoms are more prognostic than signs. [Important]
- Signs that have prognostic value are, in order severity:
- Neck tenderness < neck stiffness < neurological deficit.
- Neurological deficits "rarely conform to myotomes or dermatomes."
- Processes of pain inhibition may cause upper limb weakness and impaired reflexes.
- [KP] **The longer the whiplash-injured patients symptoms last, the worse the prognosis.**
- [KP] **In reviewing 15 studies on whiplash-injury outcomes:**
  - **Fewer than 50% of all patients made a full recovery; 4.5% were permanently disabled.**
- Gargan and Bannister's reports of consecutive series patients attending an Emergency Department showed the following:
  - 66% of whiplash-injured patients fully recover

- 2% of whiplash-injured patients are disabled
- **[KP] 12% of whiplash-injured patients who became asymptomatic by 2 months after injury will have their symptoms return by 2 years after injury.**
- 7% of whiplash-injured patients who became asymptomatic by 3 months after injury will have their symptoms return by 2 years after injury.
- **[KP] Although some whiplash-injured patients will improve over 2.5 years after injury, "improvement is minimal after the first year."**
- The symptoms associated with a worse outcome are:
  - Rapid onset of pain (2 references)
  - Severe neck pain (3 references)
  - Acute hospital admission (1 reference)
  - Radiation of pain to the upper limb (7 references)
  - Headache (1 reference)
- **[KP] "The whiplash syndrome has both physical and psychological components."**
- The psychological components of whiplash injury include:
  - Impaired concentration
  - Somatoform disorder
  - Forgetfulness
  - Post-traumatic stress disorder
  - Driving anxiety
- Whiplash-injured patients "have normal behavioral profiles early after their injury, but as the pain persists they develop psychological sequelae."
- Whiplash-injured patients may develop depressive symptoms after 6 weeks.
- The greater the whiplash-injured patient's pain, "the worse is the psychological response."
- In whiplash-injured patients, mood disorder after one year is twice that in the general population.

- Factors significantly associated with a poor outcome independent of symptoms and signs include:
  - Older age
  - Lower educational achievement
  - Part-time employment
  - Pre-existing neck and low back pain
  - Previous whiplash injury
- In whiplash-injured patients, clerical employees returned to work twice as quickly as manual workers. Self-employed were half as likely to take time off, but they took much longer to recover fully.
- Whiplash-injured patients are 5 times more likely to suffer from chronic neck pain than control populations.
- The view that a whiplash-injured patient's symptoms will improve once litigation has finished "is unsupported by the literature." (5 references)
- Litigation does not affect a whiplash-injured patient's rate of employment.
- The more severe a whiplash-injured patient's pain, the more likely they will engage in ongoing litigation.
- In the general population, neck pain is not associated with cervical spondylosis or with advancing age. **Important: this means that it is not appropriate to ascribe a whiplash-injured patient's neck pain to pre-injury spondylosis.**
- Pre-accident spondylosis doubles the probability of developing neck pain from a MVC. [**This suggests that pre-accident spondylosis reduces the ability of joints to handle the imparted forces, increasing injury and symptoms**].
- "Patients whose necks are spondylotic at the time of their accident have an incidence of pain of 53% after two years."
- [KP] **"Patients who sustain a whiplash injury in their third decade and undergo radiography ten years later show a level of cervical spondylosis which is typical of necks 15 years older."** *Important: whiplash injury accelerates cervical spondylosis by 15 years.*
- MRI disc degeneration rates are the same in symptomatic and

asymptomatic populations. **Important: again, this indicates that it is not appropriate to ascribe a whiplash-injured patient's neck pain to pre-injury spondylosis.**

- These authors downplay the significance and quality of the biosocial whiplash studies. They claim that when reviewing the most referenced biosocial whiplash studies that "a significant minority of patients who sustain a whiplash injury continue to experience long-term symptoms."

- [KP] **"For an acute whiplash injury, a soft cervical collar is less effective than normal activity, physiotherapy or Maitland's manipulations."**

- [KP] **"The use of the soft cervical collar gives worse results than that of no treatment at all, but is still widely prescribed."**

- [KP] 17% of whiplash injured patients who become **asymptomatic will have a relapse of symptoms within 3 months.**

- "Overall, treatment for a late [chronic] whiplash injury is relatively ineffective." [Interestingly, two of these authors (Bannister and Gargan) have published two studies on the chiropractic treatment of late whiplash injury with outstanding (74–93% improvement) results.]

Chiropractic treatment of chronic 'whiplash' injuries
Injury
Volume 27, Issue 9, November 1996, Pages 643–645

"The results of this retrospective study would suggest that benefits can occur in over 90% of patients undergoing chiropractic treatment for chronic whiplash injury."

A symptomatic classification of whiplash injury and the implications fortreatment
The Journal of Orthopedic Medicine
Volume 21(I), 1999, Pages 22–25

[KP] **"Chiropractic is the only proven effective treatment in chronic [whiplash] cases."**

Early mobilization of acute whiplash injuries
British Medical Journal
Vol. 292, March 8, 1986, pp 656-657
K Mealy, H Brennan, GCC Fenelon

From Abstract:

Acute whiplash injuries are a common cause of soft tissue trauma for which the standard treatment is rest and initial immobilization with a soft cervical collar. Because the efficacy of this treatment is unknown a randomized study in 61 patients was carried out comparing the standard treatment with an alternative regimen of early active mobilization.

Results showed that eight weeks after the accident the degree of improvement seen in the actively treated group compared with the group given standard treatment was significantly greater for both cervical movement and intensity of pain.

These Authors Also Note:

[KP] Rear end collisions cause soft tissue injuries of the neck. The "severity of injury depends on the degree of movement of the head and neck on the trunk and the acceleration." *Note: Severity of injury is NOT dependent on damage to the vehicle.*

[KP] Whiplash soft tissue neck "injuries frequently result in prolonged disability."

These authors examined the response of patients to the standard whiplash treatment of using a soft cervical collar and analgesia before gradual mobilization, compared with that of another group given alternative treatment of daily neck exercises and mobilization.

This study is a prospective randomized trial where 61 consecutive patients with acute whiplash injuries were randomized to receive active treatment (31 patients) or standard (cervical collar) treatment (30 patients).

The group assigned to receive active treatment received applications of ice in the first 24 hours, then neck mobilization and daily exercises of the cervical spine.

Daily exercises were performed every hour at home, within the limits of pain; no analgesia was needed for this mobilization treatment or the exercises.

"The group given standard treatment received a soft cervical collar and were advised to rest for two weeks before beginning gradual mobilization." "Four and eight weeks after the accident both groups were assessed for residual pain and cervical movement by one of us (KM), who was unaware of the patient management."

[KP] "Though pain in both groups was similar initially, pain in the group given active treatment was significantly less than that in the group given standard treatment at both four weeks and eight weeks."

[KP] "Movement increased significantly in the group given active treatment at four weeks and eight weeks." "At eight weeks movement in the group given active treatment was significantly greater than that in the group given standard treatment." *[Important: early intervention of Chiropractic, massage and physical therapy also helps increase mobility and decrease pain]*

[KP] "Many patients with whiplash injuries present late, after a period of immobility, with persistent pain and stiffness."

[KP] "We found that patients who are treated actively show significantly greater improvement in both cervical movement and intensity of pain compared with patients treated in the standard way." *[wow!]*

"At four weeks a significant increase in cervical movement occurred in the patients given active treatment but not in those given standard treatment. At eight weeks cervical movement was significantly greater in the patients given active treatment than those given the standard reatment, indicating that the increase in cervical mobility occurred earlier and to a significantly greater degree with active treatment."

[KP] "At both four and eight weeks the improvement in pain was significantly greater in the group given active treatment, so that these patients had significantly less pain at four and eight weeks compared with the patients given standard treatment."

[KP] "In conclusion, our results confirmed expectations that initial immobility after whiplash injuries gives rise to prolonged symptoms whereas a more rapid improvement can be achieved by early active management without any consequent increase in discomfort." *This highlights the importance of referring these patients to specialists in the treatment of whiplash because active care and joint mobilization help reduce pain without consequence or increase in discomfort.*

Dynamic Responses of Female and Male Volunteers in Rear Impacts

Traffic Injury Prevention

December, 2008, Vol. 9, No. 6, pp. 592–599
Astrid Linder, Anna Carlsson, Mats Y. Sevensson and Gunther P. Siegmund

Objectives: Compared to males, females have up to twice the risk of whiplash associated disorders (WAD) resulting from vehicle crashes. The present study focuses on the differences in the dynamic response corridors of males and females in low-severity rear impacts.

Methods: In this study, analysis of data from volunteer tests of females from previously published data has been performed. Corridors for the average female response were generated based on 12 volunteers exposed to a change of velocity of 4 km/h and 9 volunteers exposed to a change of velocity of 8 km/h. These corridors were compared to corridors for the average male response that were previously generated based on 11 male volunteers exposed to the same test conditions.

[4 km/h X .62 = 2.5 m/h; 8 km/hr = 5 m/hr]

[KP] Results: Comparison between the male and female data showed that the maximum acceleration of the head for the females occurred on average 10 ms earlier and was 29% higher during the 4 km/h test and 12 ms earlier and 9% higher during the 8 km/h test.

These Authors Also Note:

[KP] Whiplash "injuries most commonly occur at relatively low changes of velocity (typically <20 km/h) and in impacts from all directions, though rear impacts are the most common in the accident statistics".

[KP] "Since the end of the 1960s, epidemiological data have shown that females have a 1.4 to 3 times higher risk of sustaining whiplash injuries than males."

[KP] Also, females have 3.1 times higher risk for long-term neck injury/impairment in rear impacts compared to males.

[KP] "It is thus well established that females have a larger risk of whiplash injuries resulting from vehicle crashes compared to males." Males dominate most human volunteer dynamic response whiplash experiments.

Methods

The volunteers were seated in the front passenger seat of a 1990 Honda Accord LX four-door sedan. The rear of the Honda was struck by the front of a 1981 Volvo 240DL station wagon for the volunteer tests. The Volvo's impact speeds produced speed changes of about 4 and 8 km/h on the Honda. The Honda's passenger seat was locked in the full rear position and the initial seat back angle was set to about 27 degrees from the vertical for all tests. The head restraint was locked in the full-up position. The volunteers were restrained by a lap and shoulder seatbelt and instructed to sit normally in the seat, face forward with their head level, place their hands on their lap, and relax prior to impact. The volunteers knew an impact was imminent but could not predict its exact timing. Each volunteer underwent two tests: one each at a change of velocity of 4 and 8 km/h.

Discussion

[KP] "The results of the volunteer tests analyzed in this study showed an earlier and higher peak head x-acceleration for the females compared to the males."

[KP] In a 1996 study, 75.6% of adjustable headrests were found to be in the lowest possible position. This study shows that there are characteristic differences between the response of males and females in a low severity rear impact.

[KP] "Females are at higher risk of neck injuries at low-severity impact."

Frequency and Duration of Treatment for Whiplash Injuries

There is surprisingly little written about the duration and frequency of treatment for whiplash injuries. Individual authors have published their recommendations based upon personal experience, and a few good studies have been published primarily on the duration of treatment. This published information has appeared over a span of nearly 50 years, displaying similarities and trends that are reviewed below:

Billig, 1953

An early article concerning whiplash injuries was published in 1953 by physician Harvey Billig in the Journal of the International College of Surgeons, and titled:

Traumatic Neck, Head, Eye Syndrome
Journal of the International College of Surgeons
November 1953; 20(5): pp. 558–61

In this article Dr. Billig makes several statements concerning the duration and frequency of treatment for whiplash injuries. He notes that whiplash trauma causes pain with muscle spasm and restriction of motion in the neck and upper back, which in turn causes a ligamentous fascial contracture during the ensuing weeks causing a persistent restriction of motion. For treatment of this pathophysiology he states:

- [KP] This restriction of motion can be released with "progressive accumulative mobilization stretching."
- [KP] "This mobilization stretching usually takes several months to accomplish and is something like climbing up three stairs and sliding back two."
- [KP] This is best accomplished with "forced active rotation of the head, neck and thorax to each side."
- [KP] Initially this treatment is given three times daily, then three visits weekly, always done by a therapist.
- In all cases, "when motion is attempted past the point of restriction,

the symptoms complained of, including those radiating to the head and arm, are exacerbated, so that it is possible to guide the stretching by elicitation of symptoms and make sure that the proper directions for loosening are carried out." [KP] **Make sure a specialist is doing the mobilizing.**

- "On the basis of this line of reasoning, a carefully planned remobilization of the neck and the upper part of the back by means of progressive stretching exercises has been carried out in order to free the nerves from their constriction stimuli in their foraminal pathways through the contracted fascial ligamentous structures."

- "It has been attended with gratifying elimination of symptoms and signs."

- [KP] **"It has been noted that, once full rotatory range of motion in the neck and upper dorsal portion of the spine has been obtained, the patients become symptom free."**

- [KP] **"However, it has also been noted that if they do not continue sufficient mobilization stretching exercises to maintain the full range of motion they are subject to recurrence."**

[KP] Dr. Billig's specific comment on the duration of treatment is that it can take "several months" to achieve maximum improvement. His specific comment of frequency of treatment "initially three times daily and then three times weekly."

Seletz, 1958

In 1958, neurosurgeon Emil Seletz, MD from Beverly Hills, CA and associated with the medical school at the University of California, Los Angeles (UCLA), published in the Journal of the American Medical Association an article titled (1):

Whiplash Injuries

Neurophysiological Basis for Pain and Methods Used for Rehabilitation

In this article, Dr. Seletz comments on the frequency of the treatment of whiplash injuries, stating:

- [KP] **"Treatment must be started early and must be administered by those expertly trained in physical therapy and rehabilitation."**

- [KP] "Those patients not receiving adequate therapy will not improve and will soon become discouraged and resentful."
- "Because of continued complaints, many of these patients finally see a psychiatrist. The couch would serve a better purpose in this instance if it were equipped with a traction apparatus and supplemented by a gentle massage."
- [KP] "In reviewing the types of treatment with a number of specialists in this field, it is found that, while therapy naturally varies to suit the individual need, it consists primarily of local heat in the form of hot wet packs and cervical traction, followed by very gentle massage and manual rotations." *[Currently ice is recommended over heat in the early stages of injury, first 72 hrs to two weeks.]*
- "Local hot packs relieve the muscle spasm, increase the circulation, and frequently stop severe occipital pain and headaches."
- "The importance of a carefully planned scheme of treatment must be emphasized to the patient, and treatments must be religiously carried out daily during the first two or three weeks (and then about three times weekly), depending, of course, on the individual case."
- [KP] "Delay or faulty treatment leads to adhesions about the facets and scarring about the capsular ligaments, persistent spasm, congestive lymph edema, and fibrosis of muscles, swelling, and eventual adhesions of nerves within the nerve root canals." *[Very important!]*
- [KP] "The resultant faulty posture in neglected cases enhances the degeneration of the intervertebral discs, as well as spur formation in the lateral covertebral articulations, which on the roentgenogram has come to be known as traumatic arthritis." *[Very important!]*
- [KP] "I cannot too strongly emphasize the urgency of early and persistent therapy, always by a specialist in this field."
- [KP] "Occasionally, a patient is seen with persistent complaints of head, neck, and shoulder pain, who has had on surgical exposure persistent swelling and adhesions of several nerve roots within the dural sleeve of exit. It is most likely that early, persistent, and adequate therapy by those expertly trained in

physical medicine will prevent most patients from developing a surgical condition." This highlights the importance of combined chiropractic, massage and physical therapy.

In this article, Dr. Seletz makes no mention of duration of treatment. However, with respect to frequency of treatment, he makes two important recommendations:

- Treatment must begin early and it must be persistent.
- "The importance of a carefully planned scheme of treatment must be emphasized to the patient, and treatments must be religiously carried out daily during the first two or three weeks (and then about three times weekly), depending, of course, on the individual case."

Jackson, 1978

Historically, the most authoritative book concerning whiplash injuries is The Cervical Syndrome, authored by Ruth Jackson, MD. Dr. Jackson's credentials are impressive. She was Assistant Clinical Professor of Orthopedic Surgery at the Southwestern Medical School of the University of Texas, Consulting Orthopedic Surgeon at Baylor Medical Center, Chief of Orthopedic Surgery at Parkland Hospital, and Instructor in Orthopedic Surgery at Baylor University College of

Medicine. The fourth edition of Dr. Jackson's book was published in 1978. Relevant to duration and frequency of treatment for whiplash injuries, Dr. Jackson states (3):

- "Treatment schedules will vary somewhat for each individual."
- [KP] **"Some patients may require daily treatments for a week or two, after which the treatments should be given two or three times per week."**
- [KP] **"As the symptoms decrease the treatments can be spaced farther apart unless the patient experiences an exacerbation of symptoms, in which event more frequent treatments may be necessary."**

Once again, we have an experienced, expertly trained clinician, Dr. Ruth Jackson, noting that some patients require a treatment frequency for a week or two followed by a frequency of two or three times per week. Dr. Jackson makes no comment on duration other than to state that if there is an exacerbation of symptoms, "more frequent treatments may be necessary."

Ameis, 1986

In 1986, Arthur Ameis, MD published an article in which he comments on the duration of whiplash treatment (4). Dr. Ames practices physical medicine and rehabilitation, and is on the Faculty of Medicine at the University of Toronto. The title of his article is:

Cervical Whiplash: Considerations in the Rehabilitation of Cervical

Myofascial Injury

**Canadian Family Physician
Volume 32, September 1986**

In this article, Dr. Ameis notes:

[KP] Mild (first degree spinal myofascial strain) soft tissue injuries to the neck "may develop immediately or more slowly after injury, will heal rapidly, with minimal work time loss and a symptom-free status about six months post injury. 'Mild' may inadvertently connote the trivial." *[Grade I and II by the Croft guidelines]*

[KP] Moderate (second degree spinal myofascial strain) may develop symptoms over 24 hours. "These persons will experience serious problems with substantial work loss of weeks or months, but will recover a normal lifestyle within six months to two years." *[Grade III to V by the Croft guidelines]*

[KP] "Within one year, about 50% of patients in the 'moderate' category will have recovered to the level of 'functional recovery': a full range of activities of daily living will be restored, but often with intermittent symptoms of rheumatism in damp or cold, and intolerance of a prolonged neck position or of extreme turning or extension."

"After 18 – 24 months, almost all patients [with moderate injury] will have reached functional recovery, although some report recovery up to five years later."

"For second-degree spinal myofascial injuries, the plateau will be reached between 12 and 36 months post injury."

"15% of patients fail to achieve a full functional recovery, and some 40%–70% find some mild symptom persistence." "Severe injuries (third degree) are disabling in the very long term or even permanently."

"About 10%–15% of motor vehicle cervical injuries fail to achieve a functional recovery even after the passage of two to three years. This failure may be the result of physical impairment, minimal brain damage from head injury, or chronic pain syndrome."

[KP] "Overall, a patient with a neck injury has an 85%–90% chance of achieving a functional recovery. *[With proper treatment and rehab.]* Anywhere from 40%–70% of such patients retain some degree of intermittent, unpleasant, unnatural symptoms in the injured tissues." *[More likely without proper treatment and rehab.]*

[KP] About 50% of the more seriously injured will have recovered by the end of the first year. About 25% additionally will recover in the next 6 months (18 months since injury). About 15% will recover 18 months post injury. *Therefore, it is premature to claim that a patient has failed to recover until at least 18 months after injury, and possibly even longer.*

[KP] As noted, Dr. Ameis does not comment on the frequency of treatment. However, he had quite a bit to say about duration. Specifically, he notes that the simplest of injuries require 6 months, moderate injuries require up to two years, and occasionally some individuals require 3–5 years before they reach maximum improvement.

Gargan and Bannister, 1990

In 1990, physicians Martin Gargan and Gordon Bannister published a long-term prognosis study on whiplash victims (5). Drs. Gargan and Bannister are from the University of Bristol in the United Kingdom, and they have published a number of long-term prognosis and treatment studies pertaining to whiplash trauma. Dr. Gargan is additionally distinguished as Registrar in Accident and Emergency Surgery at John Radcliffe Hospital, Headington, England, and Dr.

Bannister is additionally distinguished as Consultant and Senior Lecturer, Department of Orthopaedic Surgery, Southmead General Hospital, Westbury-on-Trym, Bristol, England. The title of their 1990 article is:

Long-term Prognosis of Soft-Tissue Injuries of the Neck
Journal of Bone and Joint Surgery (Br)
VOL. 72-B, No. 5, September 1990

In this study, the authors reviewed 43 patients who had sustained soft tissue injuries of the neck after a mean 10.8 years. They concluded that most of the patients had reached their maximum improvement within two years of being injured. Specifically, they state:

[KP] "After two years, symptoms did not alter with further passage of time."

[KP] **Although Drs. Gargan and Bannister make no comment on the frequency of treatment, they do present a rationale for treatment to extend for two years.**

Mercy Document, 1992

In 1989, the United States federal government established the Agency for Health Care Policy and Research. "At that time the message was clear – either the health professions developed their own guidelines or third parties would impose them." (p. xxxvii)

In the chiropractic profession, the task of attempting to do something was taken up by the Congress of Chiropractic State Associations or COCSA. The COCSA has approximately 48 association representatives from approximately 40 different states. The COCSA assembled an initial steering committee of nine members. Through a slow and detailed process, the nine-member steering committee chose 35 chiropractic physicians to be participants for the commission to develop a consensus document on chiropractic quality assurance and parameters of practice. With broad support from chiropractic colleges and organizations, the 35 consensus commission members completed a long and arduous process of creating their document. The results of their efforts is commonly referred to as The Mercy Guidelines (6), or the Mercy document.

The Mercy document is 222 pages in length and it discusses essentially every aspect of chiropractic clinical practice. The suggested adoption for these guidelines was of July 1, 1993. (p. iv) Even though the literature referenced in this document almost exclusively pertain to low back issues, page xl notes that the Guidelines "apply to patients with neck pain and headache as well as low back pain."

Chapter Eight of the Mercy document is tilted: **Frequency and Duration of Care.** Page 117 of the Mercy document notes that the frequency and duration of treatment is:

[KP] "Based on the expectation of outcome for the uncomplicated case."

[KP] Additionally, page 125 notes that, "only acute episodes can truly be considered uncomplicated."

[KP] Dr. Dan Murphy's interpretation of chiropractic care for patients with musculoskeletl spine pain from reading Chapter Eight of the Mercy document, including acute whiplash trauma, is as follows:

- [KP] Treatment five days per week for the initial first two weeks
- [KP] Three times per week for the second two weeks
- [KP] Three times per week for weeks five and six, although this is vague in the document
- [KP] Two times per week for the next ten weeks

[KP] This adds up to a total treatment of 42 patient treatment visits over a period of 16 weeks for the management of an acute uncomplicated musculoskeletal problem.

[KP] Importantly, the Mercy document says that to this number (42 visits over 16 weeks), one could add in:

- Additional treatment for acute exacerbations
- Additional treatment for significant deterioration of clinical status
- Elective treatment that does not create physician dependence
- Additional treatment determined by multipliers of specific historical factors. These specific historical factors include:
    - Length of time the patient had the problem

- Severity of the symptoms
- The number of previous episodes of similar complaints
- Existence of any pre-existing complicating conditions

These historical factors are not given in a specific formula format, so the treating doctor would use them on a case-by-case basis.

The Mercy document also explains what is meant by complicated cases. Complicated cases are allowed additional treatment. This information is scattered over several pages (pp. 119, 121, 125, and 129), and are here listed:

- Inflammation of the disc, ligament or muscle
- Degenerative processes
- Intra-articular adhesions
- Meniscoid entrapments
- Occupational hazards, such as prolonged static postures and/or high peak spinal loads
- Anomalous structure
- Re-injury and exacerbation from unexpected events
- Biomechanical stress
- Spondylolithesis

[KP] By reviewing this list, it appears that many acutely whiplash-injured patients will be classified as complicated cases. The Mercy document acknowledges that such complicated cases may require additional duration and frequency of treatment. Yet, the Mercy document is vague on a formula for such additional treatment, especially if more than one factor exists.

[KP] At the minimum, it appears that the Mercy document suggests increasing treatment by 50% if one factor exists. This would increase duration to 24 weeks and the treatments to 63 visits.

[KP] There appears to be no hard application when more than one factor exists. A defensible argument would suggest a doubling of the treatment allowed for the acute uncomplicated case, which would increase duration to 32 weeks and the treatments to 84 visits. *[Sadly, these guidelines were grossly misunderstood and misused classifying all cases as "uncomplicated" limiting rehabilitation care to 12 visits or less.]*

In terms of disclosure and exceptions, the Mercy document makes the following points:

- "These recommendations do not give a 'cookbook' approach to the duration of care or number of treatments." (p. xl)
- "They are not designed as a prescriptive procedure for determining the absolute frequency and duration of treatment/care for any specific case." (p. 117)
- "No attempt has been made to select for individual conditions by region of complaint or by diagnosis."
- "Note: statistical descriptions of treatment frequency such as mean/median/mode, should NOT be used as a standard to judge care administered to an INDIVIDUAL patient." (p. 124)

Consistent with the prior references, treatment frequency begins with daily treatment for acute problems and graduates to three times and then two times per week. The Mercy Document would argue for duration between 4 months to 8 months, and possibly longer for unique individual cases.

Schofferman and Wasserman, 1994

In 1994, orthopedic surgeon Jerome Schofferman published a unique study on whiplash-injured patients, as follows (7):

Successful treatment of low back pain and neck pain after a motor
vehicle accident despite litigation
Spine
May 1, 1994;19(9):1007–10

In this study, Drs. Schofferman and Wasserman do not mention frequency of treatment, but they do document the duration of treatment required for whiplash-injured patients to achieve maximum improvement. The 39 patients in this study were acute or subacute, "not entrenched chronic pain patients." Using the standard measurement outcome tools of the McGill Pain Questionnaire the Oswestry Low Back Disability Questionnaire, these authors concluded:

- [KP] "Patients with low back pain or neck pain resulting from a motor vehicle accident showed a statistically significant improvement with treatment despite ongoing litigation."
- "Patients remained in treatment until they were pain free and functionally normal or until a permanent and stable plateau was reached despite continuing symptoms."
- Patients were treated until they became pain free, or until they reached maximum improvement. Maximum improvement was claimed after "mild to moderate pain remained stable for approximately 8 weeks."
- [KP] "The mean duration of treatment was 29 weeks [7 months 1 week]."
- [KP] The range of treatment was 8 weeks (2 months) to 108 weeks (2 years and 1 month).

The most important finding from this study is that the range for recovery for patients suffering from acute or subacute whiplash injuries is between 2 months and 2 years, with a mean of 7 months of treatment.

Barnsley, 1994

In October of 1994 the Australian research team of Leslie Barnsley, Susan Lord, and Nikoli Bogduk, published a detailed, 24 page, Clinical Review of Whiplash Injuries, as follows (8):

Whiplash Injury, Clinical Review
Pain 58, October 1994, pp. 283-307

Once again, these authors did not comment on the frequency of treatment, but they did comment on the duration of symptomology, as follows:

[KP] "75% of patients with whiplash injuries will heal spontaneously in 2-3 months. These patients sustained minor injuries to their muscles and ligaments, but not to their discs or zygapophysial joints."

[KP] "25% of patients with whiplash injuries will progress to chronic symptoms. These patients injured their intervertebral discs, zygapophysial joints, or alar ligaments. These patients will not resolve spontaneously and they do become chronic. These patients may improve over a periods of 2 years, and are unlikely to improve after 2 years."

[KP] Once again, in accordance with other studies above, duration of treatment for symptoms can span a period of a few months to two years.

Tomlinson, 2005

In 2005, British researcher P.J. Tomlinson teamed up with physicians Martin Gargan and Gordon Bannister, and published a 7.5 year prospective review on 42 whiplash-injured patients, as follows (9):

The fluctuation in recovery following whiplash injury
7.5-year prospective review
Injury
Volume 36, Issue 6, June 2005, Pages 758–761

Once again, these authors did not comment on the frequency of treatment, but they did comment on the duration of symptomology, noting the following:

[KP] "Symptoms [from whiplash injuries] largely stabilized within 3 months but there was significant fluctuation in symptom severity between 3 months and 2 years." This suggests that outcome cannot be accurately assessed during this time [during the first 3 months].

"Our results support the work of previous authors, demonstrating little alteration in symptoms by 3 months and stabilizing at 2 years."

By 7.5 years 64% of patients have the same symptom severity they had at 3 months, and in 36% their symptom status changed: 17% improved and 19% deteriorated.

[KP] "Between 3 months and 2 years symptoms fluctuate significantly and during this time any estimation of patients' prognosis will be unreliable." The cause of this fluctuation is "important in medico-legal reporting since patients' outcome can only be predicted at 3 months and not confirmed until 2 years."

Once again, in accordance with other studies noted above, duration of treatment for symptoms can span for a period of two years. [This gives good reason as to why proper and early diagnosis/treatment is so critical. Following the Croft guidelines increases outcome success.]

A summary of these articles is in the table below:

Year	Author	Duration	Frequency
1953	Billig	Several months	3x/day then 3x/wk
1958	Seletz	N/A	Start Early Daily 2–3 wks Then 3x/wk
1978	Jackson	N/A	Daily 1–2 wks Then 3x/wk
1992	Mercy Document	Uncomplicated: 16 weeks Complicated: 23–32 weeks	Daily for 2 wks Then 3x/wk for 4 wks Then 2x/wk for 10 wks =42 wks 1.5 or 2x the uncomplicated frequency
1994	Schofferman	2 mo–2yrs 1 mo Mean: 7 mo 1wk	N/A
1994	Bamsley	3 mo–2 yrs	N/A
2005	Tomlinson	3 mo–2 yrs	N/A

Croft, 2002

The greatest amount of work concerning the frequency and duration for treatment of whiplash injuries has been done by Arthur Croft, DC. The Croft Whiplash Guidelines are the most accepted and used duration and frequency guidelines for the treatment of whiplash injuries. Dr. Croft is a noted whiplash lecturer, researcher and author (10). Dr. Croft's guidelines are based on his analysis of approximately 2,000 randomly selected cases from a number of treating practitioners' files. In the chiropractic profession, Dr. Croft's Whiplash Guidelines have been adopted by many States in the US and the International Chiropractic Association.

For whiplash injuries, Dr. Croft originated 5 grades of injury which have been universally accepted, as follows:

Grades	Severity	Anatomical and Clinical Description
I	Minimal	No limitation of range of motion, no ligamentous injury, no neurological symptoms.
II	Slight	Limitation of range of motion, no ligamentous injury, no neurological findings.
III	Moderate	Limitation of range of motion, some ligamentous injury, neurological findings present.
IV	Moderate to Severe	Limitations of range of motion, ligamentous instability, neurological findings present, fracture or disc derangement
V	Severe	Requires surgical treatment and stabilization – chiropractic care post surgery.

Treatment Recommendation based on Grade:

Grades	Croft Frequency and Duration Guidelines							
	Daily	3x/wk	2x/wk	1x/wk	1x/m	Total Duration	Total Number of Visits
I	1 wk	1-2 wks	2-3 wks	4 wks		10 wks	21
II	1 wk	4 wks	4 wks	4 wks	4 mo	29 wks	33
III	1-2 wks	10 wks	10 wks	10 wks	6 mo	56 wks	76
IV	2-3 wks	16 wks	12 wks	20 wks	**	**	**
V	Surgical stabilzation necessary - Chiropractic care is post surgical.						
** May require permanent monthly or permanent palliative care								

See "Treatment Guidelines" on page 71.

References:

- Billig, Harvey, MD; Traumatic Neck, Head, Eye Syndrome; Journal of the International College of Surgeons November 1953; 20(5): pp. 558–61.

- Seletz, Emil, MD; Whiplash Injuries: Neurophysiological Basis for Pain and Methods Used for Rehabilitation; Journal of the American Medical Association; November 29, 1958, pp. 1750–1755.

- Jackson, Ruth, MD; The Cervical Syndrome; Fourth Edition, Charles C Thomas publisher, 1978, p 291.

- Ameis, Arthur, MD; Cervical Whiplash: Considerations in the Rehabilitation of Cervical Myofascial Injury; Canadian Family Physician Volume 32, September 1986.

- Gargan M. F., Bannister G. C.; Long-term Prognosis of Soft-Tissue Injuries of the Neck; Journal of Bone and Joint Surgery (British); VOL. 72-B, No. 5, September 1990.

- Mercy Document, Appleton, 1992.

- Schofferman J, Wasserman S; Successful treatment of low back pain and neck pain after a motor vehicle accident despite litigation; Spine May 1, 1994;19(9):1007–10.

- Barnsley L, Lord S, Bogduk N; Whiplash injury, Clinical Review; Pain 58, October 1994, pp. 283–307.

- P.J. Tomlinson, M.F. Gargan and G.C. Bannister; The fluctuation in recovery following whiplash injury: 7.5-year prospective review; Injury Volume 36, Issue 6, June 2005, pp. 758–761.

- Foreman SM, Croft AC Whiplash Injuries: The Cervical Acceleration/Deceleration Syndrome; 3rd edition, Philadelphia, Lippincott Williams & Wilkins, 2002, pp. 525–526

Shaken Baby Syndrome as compared to Whiplash or CAD injuries from MVCs.

Review Article

Shaken Baby Syndrome A Common Variant of Non-Accidental Head Injury in Infants

Jakob Matschke, Dr. med.,*1 Bernd Herrmann, Dr. med.,2 Jan Sperhake, Dr. med.,3 Friederike Körber, Dr. med.,4 Thomas Bajanowski, Prof. Dr. med.,5 and Markus Glatzel, Prof. Dr. med.6

There is little research data regarding children and MVCs other than death statistics. Since Shaken Baby Syndrome and MVC are both acceleration/deceleration induced injuries lets compare the data.

- SBS or non-accidental head injury (NAHI), which has high morbidity and mortality.

- Shaken baby syndrome is a common manifestation of non-accidental head injury in infancy. In Germany, there are an estimated 100 to 200 cases annually.

- The mortality can be as high as 30%, and up to 70% of survivors suffer long-term impairment.

- The shaken baby syndrome (SBS) is a common form of NAHI in which the victim is held by the torso or the extremities and violently shaken, causing abrupt uncontrolled head movements with a marked rotatory component. [**whiplash or CAD**]

- In 1971 the British neurosurgeon Norman Guthkelch described two infants with subdural hemorrhage but no signs of external injury; as the cause, he suspected an acceleration-deceleration mechanism ("whiplash injury") (e10).

- A number of anatomical features make infants particularly vulnerable to acceleration-deceleration events with a marked rotatory component, which typically occur on shaking [**and MVCs**] (2, 13–15, e38, e39). The head is large in relation to the rest of the body and is not yet adequately supported and controlled by the weak, immature neck musculature (14, e40). [**important**]

- The result is vigorous movements of the various intracranial compartments relative to one another, e.g., between the skull and dura on the one hand and the cerebral surface on the other, or between the white matter and the gray matter. Although many details remain unclear, the overwhelming majority of investigators agree that the resulting shear forces are responsible for subdural hemorrhages and diffuse brain damage (3, 14–15, e38—e44).

- "Simple" shaking without impact suffices to produce the full picture of SBS with or without fatal outcome, but the energy resulting from an **abrupt deceleration through impact is certainly higher and thus leads to more severe trauma.** This abrupt deceleration, such as what can occur in a motor vehicle collision is sometimes referred to as shaken impact syndrome.

- Neuropathological investigation has revealed signs of corresponding focal damage in the lower brainstem (e51, e52). Even if a long-lasting episode of apnea is not immediately fatal, the resulting hypoxia causes cerebral edema with increased intracranial pressure and thus reduced cerebral blood flow, leading to a vicious circle of increasing cerebral hypoxia. The end result in such cases—depending on the delay before initiation of emergency treatment—is either protracted brain death or prolonged survival with serious deficits (e53–e55). **Children with CAD injuries may not show signs for some time.** Moreover, the shear forces that act on the immature brain during shaking result in traumatic diffuse axonal injury (DAI) (e51, e52), which also participates in the development of cerebral edema (16, e56).

- For forensic purposes, it is important that in SBS—following from biomechanical and pathophysiological principles—impairment of cerebral function, or symptoms, begin immediately after the shaking event. In other words, a shaken infant who displays severe neurological symptoms at a later stage is unlikely not to have shown signs of injury straight after shaking. Furthermore, the accounts given by many confessed perpetrators describe occurrence of the symptoms immediately following non-trivial shaking (e48, e57–e59).

- Patients with SBS have a poorer prognosis than victims of serious accidents; this can be attributed in particular to the differences in mechanism of injury and the frequent delay in taking the child to a doctor (e61–e64). **Kids in MVC who do not show immediate symptoms are too often not checked by a specialist in a timely fashion.**

- Severe accidental head injuries are extremely rare in this age group and usually the result of falls from great heights or high-speed vehicle accidents (e101, e102).

- The welfare of the child must always have absolute priority. **Get kids checked immediately whether MVC or SBS.**
- Careful consideration is required in each individual case. If, after such consideration, there is the impression of serious, unavertable danger to the child's life or physical integrity.

Key Points by Dr. Shetlin

According to other pediatric trauma research…

- "The most common cause of serious pediatric spinal trauma is motor traffic incidents."
- "Traffic-related incidents accounted for approximately one third of all spinal trauma and half of serious injuries."
- Spinal injuries were classified as serious if a fracture, spinal cord injury, vertebral subluxation/dislocation, or major ligamentous injury was present. Of age groups 0–16, the 0–4-year age group had the highest proportion of serious injuries, at 47% of the group.

According to this the above research points…

- SBS is a non-accident version of a whiplash injury or CAD.
- The Mortality and Morbidity rate is the same as MVC for the age Group 0–4 years old.
- SBS has been defined as an "acceleration/deceleration or "whiplash" injury since 1971. This is the same terminology use in MVC.
- SBS and Whiplash are worse with a rotation component.
- The large head-to-body ratio combined with the immature/weak neck muscles of an infant or child make the likelihood of injury greater.
- Rapid shear forces are hazardous to neck muscles, ligaments, dura matter brain tissue, spinal and intracranial blood vasculature.
- Abrupt deceleration with impact increases chance of injury.
- Severe or visible injuries prompt parents to have children seen by a doctor sooner.
- Lower brain stem injuries may not be noticeable at first but can be fatal over time.
- Many soft tissue injuries go unnoticed for long periods of time leading to greater problems to deal with later.
- Each child's case is individual and should be checked immediately for the welfare of the child.

Pediatric Neurosurg. 2002 Nov;37(5):245-53.
Infantile subdural hematomas due to traffic accidents.

Vinchon M, Noizet O, Defoort-Dhellemmes S, Soto-Ares G, Dhellemmes P.

Department of Pediatric Neurosurgery, CHRU de Lille, Lille, France.
m-vinchon@chru-lille.fr

The most common cause of subdural hematomas (SDH) in infants is shaken-baby syndrome (SBS). The pathogenesis and natural history of infantile SDH (ISDH) are poorly documented, because in SBS, the date of shaking is usually imprecise and the assault is often repeated. Victims of traffic accidents (TA) form a study group close to experimental conditions, because the trauma is unique, witnessed and dated. We reviewed 18 cases of SDH due to TA in infants under the age of 24 months. Our goal was to investigate the clinical and radiological data and natural history of SDH. A subdural collection was found on the day of trauma in 7 cases. In 3 of these, the collection was already hypodense. The perifalcine region was the most frequent site of intracranial bleeding. Blood hyperdensity was always found on CT scans performed during the first week, and turned hypodense on about the 9th day. Three patients had retinal hemorrhage, of a type distinct from that found in SBS. Drainage of the SDH was required in 14 cases after a mean delay of 13.5 +/- 5.8 days after trauma. Four patients also required a ventriculoperitoneal shunt because of associated hydrocephalus. Our data suggest that impaired CSF drainage plays a large role in the pathogenesis of ISDH. The fact that a single and recent trauma can result in mixed-density ISDH can be of great importance in forensic medicine. Copyright 2002 S. Karger AG, Basel.

PMID: 12411716 [PubMed - indexed for MEDLINE]

Position paper on fatal abusive head injuries in infants and young children.

Case ME, Graham MA, Handy TC, Jentzen JM, Monteleone JA; National Association of Medical Examiners Ad Hoc Committee on Shaken Baby Syndrome.

Department of Pathology, St Louis University Health Sciences Center, Missouri 63104-8298, USA.

Comment in:

Am J Forensic Med Pathol. 2002 Mar;23(1):105; author reply 105-6

This article represents the work of the National Association of Medical Examiners Ad Hoc Committee on shaken baby syndrome. Abusive head injuries include injuries caused by shaking as well as impact to the head, either by directly striking the head or by causing the head to strike another object or surface. **Because of anatomic and developmental differences in the brain and skull of the young child, the mechanisms and types of injuries that affect the head differ from those that affect the older child or adult.** The mechanism of injury produced by inflicted head injuries in these children is most often rotational movement of the brain within the cranial cavity. **Rotational movement of the brain damages the nervous system by creating shearing forces, which cause diffuse axonal injury with disruption of axons and tearing of bridging veins, which causes subdural and subarachnoid hemorrhages, and is very commonly associated with retinal schisis and hemorrhages.** Recognition of this mechanism of injury may be helpful in severe acute rotational brain injuries because it facilitates understanding of such clinical features as the decrease in the level of consciousness and respiratory distress seen in these injured children. The pathologic findings of subdural hemorrhage, subarachnoid hemorrhage, and retinal hemorrhages are offered as "markers" to assist in the recognition of the presence of shearing brain injury in young children.

PMID: 11394743 [PubMed - indexed for MEDLINE]
Leg Med (Tokyo). 2007 Mar;9(2):83–7. Epub 2007 Feb 2.
Abusive head injuries in infants
and young children.
Case ME

St. Louis University Medical Center, Forensic Pathology, 3556 Caroline, St. Louis, MO 63104, USA. MCase@stlouisco.com

Abusive head injuries are among the most common causes of serious and lethal injuries in children. These injuries may result from impact or shaking or a combination of these mechanisms. **These mechanisms cause the child's head to undergo acceleration-deceleration movements which may create inertial movement of the brain within the cranial compartment.** Differential movement between the brain and skull may result in subdural and subarachnoid hemorrhages and traumatic diffuse axonal injury. This paper will discuss the unique anatomical and developmental features of the immature brain, skull, and neck which render young children particularly vulnerable to shearing injuries, the pathology of those injuries, and the mechanisms of these injuries.

Certified Professionals

Personal Injury Training Institute Graduates

http://personalinjurytraininginstitute.com/certified-motor-vehicle-collision-occupant-injury-professionals/

Spinal Research Institute of San Diego Graduates

http://www.srisd.com/graduates_states.htm

About the Author

Dr. J. Shetlin completed his undergraduate studies at Riverside CC in Southern California and at the University of Utah in Salt Lake City. Graduate studies were completed at Palmer College of Chiropractic in Davenport, IA where he received his B.S. and Doctorate Degree.

He has been passionate about health and the human body since his youth. Growing up with role models like nutrition and fitness guru - Jack LaLanne, "The Incredible Hulk" – Lou Ferrigno, Mr. America and Mr. Universe -Arnold Schwarzenegger, Gymnast – Mary Lou Retton and others. Dr. Shetlin has been amazed with what the human frame can do, how it can change shape, and how it can heal itself after a trauma.

In his youth, his mother was injured in a motor vehicle collision. Visits to the chiropractor restored her health and vitality. She had mentioned how much better she felt after visiting the chiropractic physician which left an indelible impression on Dr. Shetlin's young mind. He determined he wanted to be a chiropractic physician while in the 5th grade. During his Undergraduate studies Dr. Shetlin worked at the University of Utah hospital. He was a research assistant in the OB/GYN department aiding in studies with Lupis and Pre-eclampsia. The doctors he worked with nearly had him convinced to become an OB/GYN physician.

Southern Utah

Once his graduate requirements were complete, Dr. Shetlin opened his own practice in St. George, UT. He has never stopped learning and has been a diligent servant to his community. In his six years in practice in southern Utah, Dr. Shetlin has:

- Served as President of the Utah Spinal Research Foundation
- Served as President of the American Spinal Research Foundation
- Organized a Triathlon to fund Spinal Research
- Organized the Natural Health and Fitness Expo
- Lectured frequently on "Optimal health, naturally…without drugs and surgery"
- Headed two research studies, one on asthma, the other on multiple sclerosis
- Certified as an auto accident specialist (One of only 12 in Utah at that time.)
- Volunteer lectured on auto accident physics and injury at local high schools
- Developed his practice into a group with chiropractic physicians, medical doctors, physical therapist and massage therapists all working together for the benefit of the patient

Moving to SLC… The European Detour

In 2004 Dr. Shetlin decided to sell his practice and return to northern Utah. Interestingly, while at an International Chiropractic Continuing Education seminar in Athens, Greece, Dr. Shetlin met Dr. Hatch, from Portugal. Dr. Hatch was opening multiple clinics in Portugal and looking to bring skilled doctors to Europe. The timing was right, Dr. Shetlin's children were at a great age for an international adventure, Portugal was beautiful, and his wife was willing. So, Dr. Shetlin and his family moved to practice chiropractic and serve their church in Portugal for two years.

Here and now…

Now back in the Salt Lake Valley, Dr. Shetlin continues to serve the community to the best of his ability. Dr. Shetlin has a busy life which includes:

- Lecturing on Health topics
- Teaching Auto Accident Physics and Safety lectures for local law enforcement, fire and EMTs

- Volunteering at local High School Driver's Ed classes teaching physics and injury prevention
- Training physicians of various specialties around the world on auto accident physics applied to human occupant injury and rehabilitation
- Hosting South Jordan's annual "Community Wellness Day"

What does he do in his spare time? Family, movies, mountain biking and enjoying life.

How to Engage the Author

Dr. Shetlin is available for speaking engagements, group consulting, and individual consulting. He is also available as an expert witness in litigation cases. Please contact him at

drjay@drjayshetlin.com

For information regarding private practice please visit

www.shetlin.com

Books, audio books and other education materials are available at

www.drjayshetlin.com

Additional Books in The Conundrum Series:

Solving the Health & Wealth Conundrum

The self-help book that reshapes family health-habits while saving/making them money in the process.

Available at: www.drjayshetlin.com

NOTES

When, Where and Why to Refer Auto Accident Patients

NOTES

♦ The Personal Injury Conundrum

NOTES

NOTES

The Personal Injury Conundrum

With over 3 million whiplash injuries in the US each year, countless individuals suffer from long term/chronic pain and health problems due to improper or under diagnosis and treatment. Many MD's and DC's do not realize there are specialists in the field of Motor Vehicle Occupant Injuries. Mismanagement of a motor vehicle collision case can leave the patient with undue pain and suffering as well as make it difficult for attorneys to help victims recoup their loss and pay medical bills. Whiplash and hidden soft tissue injuries often require an interdisciplinary health care team approach. Knowing when, where and why to refer auto accident patients is a vital part in helping them receive the best care possible.

"I have witnessed and worked with chiropractic physicians for many, many years. For connective tissue or soft tissue injuries, chiropractic is simply by far and away the best method of treatment. Among all the chiropractors I know Dr. Jay Shetlin is one of the best at understanding, treating, and caring for his patients with injuries of this type."

~ Bryan A. Larson, Esq

"Based on our skilled delivery of this information [the officers] will remember and implement in the field what they have learned allowing them to become more professional and effective in our community. I am hopeful that your message will be made available to hundreds of other law enforcement officers."

~ BL Smith, Training Coordinator, Sandy City Police Department

"I highly recommend your presentation and book to anybody that deals with automobile accidents.

I like the way you relate to the students and keep them actively involved. The students really appreciate your sense of humor when dealing with a delicate subject matter and are better prepared to drive on the road because of the time spent with you."

~ David Peck -Driver Education Dept. Head, Bingham High School

Whiplash and Hidden Soft Tissue Injuries